Sermons
The Pe

Wana T. Archer, PhD

Sermons that Change Lives: The Persuasive Sermon

Copyright © 2014 by Wana T. Archer

ISBN-13: 978-1495207778

ISBN-10: 1495207773

Unless otherwise noted, all scripture quotations are from the Holy Bible, King James Version, with language modernization by the author.

Monroe's Motivated Sequence from Douglas Ehninger, *Principles and Types of Speech Communication*, 9th Edition, 1986, Scott Freeman Company, Glenview, Illinois.

Illustrations, anecdotal stories, humor, and quotes are mined from fifty years of preaching. Credit is given within the text wherever possible.

Editing by Lauren Dykstra

Clip Art from Microsoft Word 2010

Dedication

To Sammie
My High School Sweetheart
Beloved Wife
My Constant and Loyal Friend
Mother of Our Three Wonderful Children
My Partner in the Grand Adventure of Ministry

The Indispensable One

About the Author

Dr. Wana Archer lives in Tulsa, Oklahoma, with his wife, Sammie. He is semi-retired after 47 years as a Baptist minister. He served congregations in Illinois, Ohio and Oklahoma.

Archer is a graduate of Southern Illinois University, Edwardsville, Southwestern Baptist Theological Seminary, and Ohio State University, where he received a PhD degree in leadership/adult education. He has an extensive educational background in speech and mass communication.

For several years Dr. Archer maintained the internet website, *Sermonhandbook.com*, which provided preaching resources for ministers.

He is currently active in the Tulsa Metro Baptist Network, a Tulsa area association of churches. He and his wife are members of South Tulsa Baptist Church, Tulsa, Oklahoma.

Author's Introduction

Get ready for a reading experience that will transform your understanding of biblical preaching and teaching. This book offers new insights into the ancient art of proclaiming the Bible.

You will discover a preaching/teaching method that, under the guiding hand of God, will help you get the results for which you have been hoping and praying. Time after time human needs will be met as the spiritual power of your preaching/teaching impacts the listener.

Sermons that Change Lives contains the knowledge ministers and teachers need to present life-changing messages. It explains and then demonstrates how topical, expository, and narrative sermons or lessons, can be written in the new persuasive sermon form. It's a new and refreshing concept. Learn it, use it, and it will become an indispensable tool for fruitful preaching and teaching.

In addition, the book is rich with inspirational illustrations and sermonic examples.

Preface

The purpose of this book is to explain and then demonstrate with model sermons how a minister may write topical, expository, and narrative sermons in the new persuasive sermon form.

Not every sermon is persuasive in purpose. But many sermons are intended to persuade the listener to act upon the truths presented in its message. Biblical truths were written to be applied. The writers of Holy Scripture called on those who read and heard the word of God to take action. They expected lives to be transformed by God's word.

Three assumptions are made by the author when explaining how a sermon may be written in the new persuasive sermon form.

1. That the person who writes a sermon in the persuasive form is a Christian; i.e., a person who acknowledges Jesus Christ as Lord and Savior.

2. That the person who writes a sermon in this sermon form does so under the leadership of the Holy Spirit.

3. That the source of the sermon in the persuasive form is the Bible. The Bible is the authoritative word of God. The sermon in the persuasive form should uncover and apply the truths of the Bible.

Preaching that utilizes this form is authoritative preaching. The speaker has confidence that the listener can apply the truths of Holy Scriptures to resolve a life need or problem.

TABLE OF CONTENTS

Section 1: The Persuasive Sermon

Section 2: 10 Persuasive Sermons for Special Days

SECTION ONE

The Persuasive Sermon

Chapter 1
Choosing the Right Sermon Form

Your alarm jolts you out of an uneasy sleep. It's Sunday morning again. The house is quiet. The rest of the family will not be up for another hour. You slip out of bed and your feet search for the soft warmth of your house slippers. Then you shuffle your way to the kitchen to put on the coffee.

With the coffee brewing, you start toward the bathroom and the ritual of washing and brushing. It's all reflexive to this point, an automaton following encoded instructions. The splash of cold water on your face elevates your consciousness. You run a hand through a tangle of unruly hair and stare at the face in the mirror.

Every seven days it happens. In approximately four hours a gathering of your congregation will be staring up into that face; yes, that face in the mirror.

They'll be waiting for you to tell them that the God of the universe still loves them; that he wants to help them with their tangled, troubled, and sometimes traumatized lives.

The Sunday sermon is written and on your desk. You'll go over it again as you sip your first cup of coffee. Perhaps you will scribble some last minute thoughts in the margins. Then you'll pray over it.

When the time comes you'll preach the prepared message and give it your best effort. But sometimes it isn't over with the last "Amen." There are those times, especially on Monday mornings, when a nagging thought won't leave you alone. Why didn't you see the decisions you had hoped for and prayed for? Why?

If that's where you are in your preaching ministry, then you and this book are on the same page. *Sermons That Change Lives* is written to get you into and through the preaching experience with the best possible results.

It's designed to bring you to the conclusion of the preaching experience knowing that God has met human needs and helped resolve human struggles.

Let's begin.

Sermon Form

Preacher, do you have a tool box? Of course you do. Every person has a few tools to maintain, repair, and build things around the house. You have specific tools for special tasks.

Now, check out your sermon tool box. How many sermon forms do you have in your sermon tool box? The sermon form is the tool that's used to build the sermon. It's the skeletal structure upon which the content of the sermon is arranged. It serves as the blueprint for the sermon, the roadmap for getting from the introduction to the conclusion of the message.

Just as the skeletal structure is vital to effective human action, so the sermon form is vital to the effectiveness of a sermon. The sermon form is one of the most important tools to help the preacher accomplish the purpose of his message.

Choosing the Right Sermon Form

Most preachers probably have one basic sermon form that is used for most sermons. Somewhere along the way to becoming a preacher, the minister learned how to shape the message for those who came to hear.

How did you decide on the sermon form that you're presently using?

It may be the speech form that you learned in a college course on public speaking. That was my case. I was a speech major at university and quickly grasped the significance of using a speech form for public speaking. The form I chose was a common one (introduction-body-conclusion).

It might be the one learned in a preaching course at seminary. I was delighted when the sermon form that I carried from university to seminary was confirmed and refined by the seminary experience. It seemed to be what the seminary professors expected and wanted.

It could be the sermon form you learned from a fellow minister. It might also be a sermon form you learned from a book on preaching.

Traditional Sermon Form

Does this look like the sermon form you're presently using? It's a common sermon form that ministers have been using for decades.

Title: Name of the sermon
Scripture: Focus of the sermon
Purpose of Sermon: The desired outcome for the sermon

Introduction to the Sermon

1. Gain attention
2. Introduce subject of the sermon

Body of the Sermon

1. Present and explain first truth
   a. Present supporting information
   b. Present additional supporting information

2. Present and explain second truth
   a. Present supporting information
   b. Present additional supporting information

3. Present and explain third truth
   a. Present supporting information
   b. Present additional supporting information

(Add scriptures, illustrations, quotes, statistics, etc., to the
   sermon points as needed)

Sermon Conclusion

1. Summarize the sermon
2, Make application
3. Invitation

This sermon form (the outline just presented) may have
served you well. It may be as comfortable as an old pair of
house shoes. Good! Keep using it. It's a valuable preaching tool.

Limits of Traditional Sermon Form

However, the traditional sermon form isn't designed (and
designed is the crucial word) to carry persuasive sermon
content.

The traditional sermon outline above seems most effective
when delivering information, or explanation, or instruction. For
example, the sermon purpose might be to define what Christians
are to believe, or to explain the meaning of a passage of
scripture, or to instruct Christians about the biblical basis for
giving.

But this sermon form isn't the right form to use when the
purpose of the sermon is persuasive; i.e., when you're asking
listeners to take action to solve a problem or meet a need.

This is an important consideration. After all, we preachers often seek to persuade worshippers to take an action to meet a need, or to solve a problem. We try to give them sound biblical reasons for doing what we ask.

We ask listeners to trust Christ and join the church in almost every Sunday morning sermon. We ask them to pray more, read the Bible more, give more, witness more, love more, serve more, etc. We ask them to change behaviors that are contrary to God's clear standards of conduct. Many Sunday morning sermons are intended to be persuasive.

Wrong Sermon Form

What happens when the content of a sermon that's intended to be persuasive is delivered in a sermon form that isn't persuasive in structure? An example is the common sermon form previously described.

Imagine trying to drive a nail into a piece of lumber with a screwdriver. You may or may not get the nail driven into the wood. The nail may bend. It may fly out of the wood. You might even break the screwdriver. In the same way, when the wrong tool is used for a persuasive sermon (the wrong sermon form) the sermon purpose may not be accomplished. The sermon application may miss the mark with disappointing results.

It's analogous to expecting a row boat (the non-persuasive sermon form) to perform as well as a tug boat (the persuasive sermon form) when trying to bring a ship into harbor. The row boat won't do as well as the tug, even though they're both boats.

Or again using the analogy of the tool box; you shouldn't expect a screwdriver to accomplish the same task as a hammer just because they're both tools.

14

Why Some Sermons Fail

The non-persuasive form may be effective for delivering some kinds of sermons; however, it's not specifically designed to carry persuasive content and secure listener response.

If persuasive sermon content is arranged in a non-persuasive sermon form it may fail at four critical points:

1. The purpose of the sermon may not be clearly defined. Persuasive sermons are always written to meet a need or solve a problem. The persuasive sermon form described in this book clearly lays out the sermon purpose and keeps the message on track to accomplish that purpose.

2. The sermon may lack a defined structure that leads to the accomplishment of the sermon purpose. This may be the greatest weakness in the non-persuasive sermon form.

The persuasive sermon form is specifically designed for persuasive sermon content. It arranges the content to best serve the sermon purpose. Each part of the persuasive form is a step toward the realization of the sermon goal.

3. The conclusion of the sermon may not reinforce its persuasive purpose. The persuasive sermon structure moves the message seamlessly and sequentially to a sermonic conclusion that is in harmony with the sermon goal of listener response.

4. The call for action at the conclusion of the sermon may be vague or indecisive. The persuasive form reinforces the sermon purpose in the call for action.

Worshipers understand what is being asked of them. They also understand why it's being asked. They understand the importance of responding to the sermon purpose.

The use of a persuasive sermon form for a persuasive sermon weds the form of the sermon to the function of the sermon. This will secure the very best possible listener response.

Helping Sermons to Succeed

The sermon form presented in this book is a marriage of form and function. It is designed to help the preacher realize the sermon purpose every time.

How is this accomplished? The persuasive form utilizes the psychology of persuasion, i.e., the way people think about problem solving.

A persuasive sermon, arranged in the persuasive form, is written to explain and resolve a perceived problem or need that the messenger has chosen to address. The problem or need may be personal to the listener or a problem or need in the church or community. The persuasive sermon, in the persuasive form, is designed to awaken the listener's interest in the perceived problem or need, and then to explain why it's important to resolve the issue.

Once the problem is defined the persuasive sermon, arranged in the persuasive sermon structure, presents a clearly defined biblical solution to the problem or need. It also includes a powerful visualization step to show the audience what might happen to the problem or need if the solution is adopted.

Lastly, the persuasive sermon calls upon the listener to act on the biblical solution presented in the sermon. It's the natural conclusion to the sermon. Isn't that what every speaker wants?

Chapter 2
Persuasive Sermon Form Explained

What exactly is the persuasive sermon form? The persuasive sermon form is an adaptation of Alan H. Monroe's motivated sequence.

Monroe was a professor at Perdue University. He was a pioneer in the liberal arts field of communications. He developed the first college course in public speaking for Perdue University.

Monroe developed a structure for creating persuasive speech in the mid-1930s. It was called the motivated sequence. It was a technique that followed the psychology of persuasion, i.e., the way people think about problem solving. The sequence is intended to inspire people to take action.

Many universities and colleges use speech textbooks that contain Monroe's motivated sequence. I first encountered Monroe's motivated sequence while teaching speech at a community college.

The Five Steps of the Motivated Sequence

A. Attention: Secure the attention of the audience. This may be accomplished through a question, dramatic story, humorous story, quotation, statistics, etc.

B. Present the Problem: Show the audience that a significant problem exists and needs resolution.

C. Present the Solution: Show that there's a solution to the significant problem being presented.

D. Visualize the Solution: Demonstrate to the audience what will happen when the solution is applied.

E. Call for Action: Tell the audience what action they can personally take to resolve this significant problem.

The Persuasive Sermon Form

The persuasive sermon form is an adaptation of Monroe's motivated sequence. There are nine steps in the adaptation. These nine steps form the persuasive sermon structure. They are divided into three groups of three.

The three groups of three steps, utilize the three basic speech divisions with which most ministers are familiar; introduction, body, and conclusion.

Three steps of the persuasive sermon form are under each main division heading in the structure: three steps under the sermon introduction, three steps under the body of the sermon, and three steps under the sermon conclusion. These nine subdivision steps are the persuasive sermon form.

Structure and Explanation of the Persuasive Sermon

The three basic divisions of the persuasive sermon form are introduction, body, and conclusion. There are three subdivision points under each basic speech division. These nine subdivision points comprise the persuasive sermon form. They are identified in the sermon structure by the alphabetical letters, A through I.

Introduction to the Sermon

A. Step One: Goodwill

It's important for the minister to draw the congregation to himself in a favorable way. He may want to comment on the weather and the joy of seeing so many present. He may comment on the significance of the day in the church calendar. He may want to introduce special guests, or perhaps a newly married couple, or a new baby, etc.

A few moments taken to introduce warmth and friendliness into the sermon time will incline the listener to hear what the minister has to say.

B. Step Two: Pre-invitation

It's the tradition of many evangelical churches to conclude the worship service with an invitation to faith in Christ and church membership. The pre-invitation is designed to prepare the listener for this concluding part of the worship service.

The minister informs the audience that the sermon will conclude with an invitation to faith in Christ and church membership. This removes the uncertainty about the conclusion of the sermon. It also permits the listener valuable time to contemplate a response to the invitation to faith and membership.

Early on in the development of the persuasive sermon form a minister friend of mine read a preliminary copy of the work. He decided to try the pre-invitation.

Three weeks later he called me excitedly to say,

"Wana, I used the pre-invitation and I've had 15 additions to the church family in the last three weeks!"

Presenting the Pre-Invitation

For example, at the time of the pre-invitation the minister might say:

"There will be an invitation to church membership at the conclusion of the service. During the invitation hymn I will be at the front (as might the other ministers on staff) to receive you and assist you."

He might add (according to each church's tradition), "If you are a baptized believer in the Lord Jesus Christ, then please come forward at that time. Allow us the joy of welcoming you into this loving fellowship."

Then, he might say, "Some of you may want to choose this wonderful Sunday to confess Jesus Christ as your Lord and Savior. You may come forward and we will joyfully receive you. We will arrange for your baptism into this fellowship."

The Primary Sermon Purpose

Of course, the primary purpose of the sermon may not be that of calling the unsaved to Christian faith. The target audience for most sermons is the church family. The purpose of the sermon may be to call upon the church member to meet a personal need, or perhaps a problem facing the church or community.

If this is the case, and it usually is, then the application (purpose) of the sermon will have two aims. The first goal is to complete the sermon in a way that accomplishes the sermon purpose for the target audience, the church family. The second goal is to transition into a call to salvation and church membership for non-members, thus concluding the invitation.

The Sermon Application

Many preachers wrestle with this problem. They will deliver excellent content in a sermon. Then, at the point of application, the time for calling the audience to respond to the sermon purpose, they will be diverted into an appeal for something else, for salvation and membership, etc. Or the message may even be concluded without any clear call for response to the sermon content and purpose.

The sermons in this book are written to demonstrate how the persuasive sermon structure can accomplish the primary sermon purpose for the target audience, and also the invitation to salvation and membership for non-members.

Further explanation of the sermon application is presented under the "G" and "H" steps of the persuasive sermon form.

C. Step Three: Attention

The minister may use an appropriate question to gain the listener's attention for the sermon. He may tell a dramatic or humorous story. He might give statistics relating to the problem he wishes to discuss. He might share a pertinent quote.

The minister might also gain the attention of the audience by asking them to turn to the scripture passage that will be the subject of the sermon.

Body of the Sermon

The exposition of the scripture passage occurs in the "Body" section of the sermon. It's this exposition that reveals the scriptural solution to the problem or need presented in the persuasive sermon.

D. Step Four: Problem/Need to be Resolved

The minister asks the congregation to turn to the passage of scripture that speaks to the problem or need to be resolved. The problem or need to be presented to the listeners may come from any one of several sources. It may have arisen from the minister's scripture study, or from his readings, or from current events.

The subject of the persuasive sermon may come from an observation of human nature, etc. The minister has become aware of a problem or need and he has chosen to address it in the sermon to the congregation.

The minister shows the listener that the problem exists. He explains why it's important to resolve the problem or need. He then gives the listener the hope that there is an answer to the problem.

E. Step Five: Solution to the Problem/Need

The congregation is invited to follow the minister's exposition or teaching of the selected scripture passage that addresses the problem.

God's solution is revealed in the exposition of the scripture passage. The solution is specific and answers the need awakened in the listener. The minister shows that the problem has a resolution that is revealed in God's word.

F. Step Six: Visualization of the Solution

The visualization of the solution is a powerful step. It helps the audience see what may happen if the scriptural answer is adopted.

The minister can draw upon a number of resources for the visualization. He might choose to use scriptural illustrations, or case studies, or human interest stories, or even personal experiences. He chooses that which will be the most appropriate to help the listener visualize the solution.

Sermon Conclusion

The minister begins to bring the sermon to a conclusion by reviewing or summarizing the main points of the message. He then completes the sermon by calling for a response to the message.

G. Step Seven: Call for Response

The minister explains to the audience what response he believes that God would have them make to the sermon. The language stating the desired action is focused, without ambiguity.

H. Step Eight: Invitation

The invitation calls on the listener to adopt the biblical solution of the sermon. The commitment is consistent with the sermon purpose.

The minister may do this by inviting listeners to come to the altar. He might ask them to stand at their seats in decision. He may ask them to complete a decision card and to bring it to the altar, or place it in the offering plate. The sermon purpose will influence the kind of invitation that's planned for the sermon completion.

Transition

When the primary purpose of the sermon has been accomplished the minister then presents the post-invitation appeal to faith in Christ and church membership. Examples of how this may be accomplished are illustrated in the model sermons and in the ten sermons of section two.

I. Step Nine: Afterglow

The minister closes the service with brief and appropriate words to the congregation which signals his warm regard for them. He may pray for them or bless them to conclude his part in the service.

Planning Beyond the Sermon

The minister should also think beyond the call for response and invitation. How may the minister and the church help the member to fulfill his or her commitment?

Perhaps it's the first Sunday of a new year. The minister has asked the listener to commit to a program to read the Bible through in the coming year. A follow up might include a Bible reading plan, periodic encouragements, and then recognition at year end.

Perhaps the minister has asked listeners to commit to sharing their faith with others. What follow up program might be developed to accomplish this sermon purpose?

You and the Persuasive Sermon Form

Ministers who decide to use the persuasive sermon form will adapt these nine steps to their own unique preaching styles.

Adapting the persuasive sermon form is analogous to the diverse appearance of each human being. Each person has the same basic skeletal structure but is unique in appearance because of the distribution of muscle, tissue (fat), and skin on the frame.

The persuasive sermon form is the skeletal structure. The sermon content is what each minister puts on the frame. How the sermon is presented is also part of the minister's adaptation.

Chapter 3
Field Tests of the Persuasive Sermon Form

The persuasive sermon form evolved over a period of several years. It assumed its present form in 2008.

I was invited on June 29, 2008, to preach at Southwood Baptist Church in Tulsa, Oklahoma for Sunday morning and evening. A sermon in the traditional sermon form was used at the morning worship service. There were no visible results at the conclusion of the sermon.

An old sermon (model topical sermon in Chapter 5) that was persuasive in content, but had been written in the common sermon form, was rearranged into the nine steps of the new persuasive sermon structure for the evening service.

The sermon was presented to an audience of about 100 adults that evening. Approximately a third of the congregation responded to the invitation and came to the altar.

After the service concluded, a young woman stood in the isle waiting to speak to me. As I approached her she reached out and took my hand.

"God sent you here tonight," she said. "I came to this service with my mind made up to end my marriage. My husband is not a bad man, but I had decided I didn't want to be married anymore."

"That's no longer the case," she added tearfully. "God spoke to me tonight. I'm going home to make my marriage work. Thank you." And with that she turned and walked away.

Field Test Results

I used sermons written in the persuasive sermon form almost exclusively for the next five years in a variety of church settings and for a variety of occasions.

Some of the sermons were my older sermons in the common form that had yielded moderate to little visible results. Rearranged into the persuasive form they proved to be much more effective.

The results were undeniable. Listeners recognized personal problems and needs. They responded to biblical solutions. The sermons were concluded with the sermon purpose being realized for many of the listeners.

There was success with both large and small church audiences. Some churches were traditional, some were contemporary. Some of the churches were plateaued or declining. Some churches were new and growing congregations.

In some of the churches the attendees were mostly older members. In some of the churches the attendees were a mix, with the majority being young to middle-aged adults.

The effectiveness of the persuasive sermon form doesn't seem to be limited by a certain size or type of audience. Interestingly, some of the most amazing results occurred in churches averaging less than 100 in Sunday school and worship.

The most important variables for the success of the persuasive sermon form seem to be the timeliness of the problem or need, and the clarity of the biblical solution being presented.

Chapter 4
How to Write a Persuasive Sermon

A persuasive sermon is always focused on resolving a problem or need. The subject of the persuasive sermon often arises from the minister's personal Bible study. It may also grow out of pastoral concerns about current events, or about church needs, or about human problems.

The minister then engages in several steps to build a persuasive sermon abstract. The sermon abstract is the blueprint that guides the sermon building process.

Create the Sermon Abstract

The reader will note that all the sermons in the book are preceded by a sermon abstract. The sermon abstract is the result of the minister's preparation. It's the road map, the blueprint, the path to the writing of the persuasive sermon.

Step One: Uncover a problem or need that will become the focus of your persuasive sermon.

Step Two: Select a passage of scripture that will address the problem or need.

Step Three: Perform an exegetical study of the scripture passage. This distills the biblical truths that will be applied to resolve the problem or need of the sermon.

Asking and answering the following questions about the text of the sermon will be helpful in creating the sermon abstract. The resultant study notes will also be valuable in building the sermon.

1. Who wrote the selected passage of scripture?

2. When was it written?

3. Who was the intended audience for the scripture passage?

4. What was the writer's purpose?

5. What is the larger context of the selected passage?

6. What is the essential meaning of key words and phrases found in the passage?

7. What light do other scriptures shed on the meaning of the passage?

8. What do other preachers and commentators say about the passage?

9. After thorough study, what is your conclusive understanding of the scripture passage?

Step Four: Prepare the sermon abstract.

1. List the central truth/s of the selected passage.

2. Write an explanatory statement that clearly defines the problem or need to be resolved.

3. Use the central truth/s of the scripture passage to write a statement that will explain the scriptural solution to the problem or need.

4. Write a purpose statement that explains the goal of the sermon.

Write the Persuasive Sermon

Use the sermon abstract as a blueprint to build your message. Utilize the nine steps of the persuasive sermon form.

1. Refine the statement that explains the need or problem that will be presented to the audience.

2. Refine the statement that explains the scriptural solution to be presented to the listeners.

3. Refine the statement that explains the response that will be asked of the audience.

4. Determine how you will help the audience visualize the scriptural solution.

5. Determine how the call for response and invitation will be presented to accomplish the sermon purpose.

6. Flesh out the sermon with scriptures, illustrations, quotes, statistics, etc., as needed.

7. Determine what (if any) follow up there will be to the sermon.

8. Then complete the three steps of the sermon introduction. Give special consideration to how the sermon will transition from the "Attention" step to the "Body of the Sermon."

9. Make use of sermon prompts. These are the signs along the sermon path that guides from point to point. I have found that words such as transition, review, summary, application, illustration, question, humor, quote, etc. are helpful.

10. Write the appropriate afterglow to conclude the sermon time.

11. If possible, record and listen to the message. Critique and refine it.

Conclusion

The model sermon in Chapter 5 visualizes the nine steps of the persuasive sermon. It demonstrates how the scripture text is applied to resolve the problem or need presented to the congregation.

This sermon was presented at the Immanuel Baptist Church, (now a satellite of FBC, Broken Arrow, Oklahoma), in Coweta, Oklahoma, on Sunday morning, September 7, 2008.

Of the approximately 100 who attended, about 40 responded to the invitation. One gentleman, who was in his fifties, came to me personally saying that he needed to turn his life around. I discovered that he was attending for the first time at the invitation of his neighbor. He hadn't been in a church service for many years. He quite happily made his confession of faith in Christ that day.

A couple in their late-fifties came back to the Lord in re-dedication of their inactive Christian lives. They too, were just visiting the church with friends. Several weeks later they joined South Tulsa Baptist Church, Tulsa, Oklahoma.

It's always a joy to see people respond to God's word with life-changing decisions. That's the purpose of the persuasive sermon.

Please note that the persuasive sermons in this book use an outline structure that is more manuscript than outline. This is the author's sermonic style.

Chapter 5
Model Topical Sermon

Sermon Abstract

Title: How do we turn lemons into lemonade?

Scripture: Matthew 5:41

Central Truth of the Scripture

Jesus tells us that there is a biblical principle that can turn life's lemons into lemonade. It is the principle of going the second mile.

Two examples of Jesus teach us the meaning of the second mile. It is the spirit of humility and kindness. It's concern for others. It's self-sacrifice. It's continuing to love even when it is hard to love.

Problem/Need to be Resolved

People are overwhelmed with personal problems; problems in families, problems in relationships, problems at work and school. Christ can help us resolve these problems through the principle of the second mile.

Solution to the Problem/Need

Jesus teaches that the principle of the second mile is a way to deal with life's overwhelming problems. It can turn lemons into lemonade.

Sermon Purpose

To encourage listener to follow the spirit of the second mile in redeeming difficult or lost situations

Introduction to the Sermon

A. Create Goodwill

God has given us a beautiful day to gather and worship. I'm so glad to see you. I have been thinking about you all week. I have been remembering some of you in prayer, because I know you are going through difficult times. I believe God has given us a special word for you this morning.

B. Explain the Pre-Invitation

At the conclusion of the message this morning, there will be a hymn of invitation. I will step down to the front of the sanctuary to welcome and assist those of you who desire to unite with this good church by transfer of membership.

Some may want to use this occasion to make a public confession of faith in our Lord Jesus Christ. We will joyfully receive you and arrange for your baptism.

Now, I know that there are many reasons why we are here today. Would you grant me one request? God has promised to be with us. Would each of you be open to hear His voice? Thank you.

Please turn in your Bibles to Matthew 5:41. This scripture is from Jesus' "Sermon on the Mount."

If someone forces you to go one mile, go with him two miles.

C. Attention

I believe this verse contains a biblical principle that, if applied, could make our lives better in almost every way.

Explain the Scripture Passage

In the days of Jesus, the Roman Empire ruled Israel. The Romans had a law that forced ordinary citizens of a ruled territory to perform menial tasks. For instance, a Roman soldier could require an ordinary citizen to carry his knapsack or equipment for a mile.

Now imagine these two scenarios.

A Roman soldiers is passing through an Israelite village. The soldier beckons to a youth to pick up his knapsack and carry it for a mile. The young man complies. The Roman probably thinks the young man despises him, so they say nothing and walk along in silence. The young man has his head down, but his eyes are searching for the mile marker at the edge of town. When he reaches it, he deposits the knapsack on the ground. He turns, and with a sullen look at the Roman soldier, silently walks back to the village.

Now, consider how this scenario might have gone if this young Israelite had followed the teaching of Jesus about going the second mile:

The youth picks up the knapsack and walks with the Roman. There is silence as they walk along. Then the youth looks at the Roman and smiles. He says, "Where is your home? Do you have family there?"

The Roman is startled by this act of civility. He answers, glad for some conversation to break the monotony of the march. They continue to converse until the mile marker is reached. But the young man continues beyond the marker, still engaging the Roman in friendly conversation. They walk together for another mile.

Then, the youth hands the knapsack to the soldier, and with a farewell salutation, says "Shalom."

Summary

Quickly note two things about this verse.

First, life sometimes gives us lemons. That is what Jesus meant when he said, "If someone forces you to go one mile..." Sometimes life happens to us and there's not much we can do about it.

But second, Jesus said, *"...go with him two miles."* Jesus is teaching us that when life happens to us, i.e., when life gives us lemons, we are to make lemonade.

Review

The principle is this; bad things happen to us. But when they do, we can go the second mile. We can act in the right way. It is this principle that turns a life situation on its head.

Humor

It also helps to smile and have a sense of humor while you are going that second mile. A man was driving down a country lane when a frog hopped into the middle of the road. He swerved, just missing the frog. He looked back in his rear view mirror and saw the frog hunkered down in the road. He parked the car on the shoulder and walked back to the frog.

He gently picked up the frog and carried it the shoulder of the road. When he sat it down, the frog spoke.

The frog said, "As you can tell, I am no ordinary frog. I have unusual powers. You have shown me this kindness. Is there something I can do for you?"

"As a matter of fact there is," said the man. "I have my old dog in the car with me. He used to be a show dog and won many blue ribbons. Now he's just old. I would love to see him be a winner just one more time."

"Show me the dog," said the frog. The man retrieved the dog from the car. It was a sad sight. The dog had only three legs. A chunk had been bitten out of one ear. The tail looked as though it had been broken in two places.

The frog studied the dog and said, "I don't think even I can help your dog. Is there something else I can do for you?"

The man thought for a moment, and then he said, "As a matter of fact there is. In two weeks I will be attending my twentieth high school reunion. I would love to be the handsomest and most successful man in my class."

The frog asked, "How tall are you?

"I'm 5 foot, 5 inches tall," said the man.

"How much do you weigh," asked the frog?

"I weigh 300 pounds," answered the man.

The frog pointed a frog foreleg at the man's head, and said, "Is that really your hair?"

"No," said the man, "it's a wig. I've been bald for years."

"Are you married?" asked the frog.

The man answered, "I was, but now I'm divorced, for the fifth time, as a matter of fact."

"What do you do for a living?" asked the frog, hopefully.

The man replied, "I'm an auditor for the IRS."

The frog studied the ground for a few seconds, and then said, "Could I take another look at the dog?"

Application

We all know there is no magical frog that can help us with the lemons of life. But I propose that the scripture that we read, "If someone forces you to go one mile, go with him two miles," if properly understood, is a piece of golden wisdom that can lead you to transform the lemons of your life into lemonade.

Body of the Sermon

D. Problem/Need to be Resolved

Let's face it friends. Jesus was preaching this sermon to people who needed help. Life had forced many unpleasant things upon them.

Have things changed in two thousand years? Are we handling life, or is life handling us? Do we need help in our personal lives? What about relationships? Do we need help in our families? What about school or work? Are there some lemons that need to be turned into lemonade today?

E. Solution to the Problem/Need

How do we turn lemons into lemonade? How does the principle of going the second mile work? How do we become a two-mile person?

Illustrations

Let me illustrate the principle of the second mile by two examples from the life of Jesus.

The first example occurred when Jesus gathered with his disciples to eat the Passover Meal on the night before his crucifixion. These men had been with Jesus for three years.

They had seen his love and kindness. They had heard his messages of hope and redemption. So, what were they doing that evening? They were arguing about who would have the preeminence and power when Jesus established his kingdom!

What did Jesus do? He applied the principle of going the second mile. Jesus got up and put a towel around his waist. He got a bowl of water and began to wash the disciple's dirty feet.

They were astonished and humiliated. Their Lord and master had assumed the role of a servant while they argued about who would be the greatest in the coming kingdom.

Jesus showed a spirit of humility and kindness. He struck a telling blow against the human inclination to demand rights and exercise power. He told the disciples that he who would be greatest in the kingdom must become a servant of others.

The second example occurred when Jesus was dying on the cross. Some of those watching called out, "If you are the Son of God, come down from the cross!"

What did Jesus do? He stayed on the cross.

He prayed, "Father, forgive them for they do not know what they are doing." Jesus went the second mile.

Jesus exercised personal forgiveness for those who had brutalized him. He remained on the cross, thus providing eternal forgiveness for all of us. Jesus struck a telling blow against those who are hard and unforgiving.

Application

We see the spirit of going the second mile in these two illustrations. The spirit is one of humility and kindness. It's concern for others. It's self-sacrifice. It's continuing to love even when it is hard to love.

37

Illustration

A minister was in the Pullman car of a train. There was a father in the Pullman car with a small baby. The infant kept crying and keeping everyone awake. The minister felt like asking the father to take the baby out, but he restrained himself.

Then, a man called out: "Mister, why don't you take that baby to its mother and let the rest of us get some sleep?"

The father replied, "I wish I could, but I can't, because the baby's mother is in a casket in the baggage car ahead."

There was silence. Then, the shuffling sound of someone walking could be heard. The man who had called out came and knelt by the father's berth.

He said, "I didn't realize that the baby's mother was dead, and that with a broken heart you were doing the best you could with the baby. Forgive me, and let me take care of the baby while you get some sleep."

This story helps us understand that the second mile spirit is one of kindness, patience, forgiveness and action.

Review

Can we again review the two aspects of this verse? Sometimes life gives you lemons. But Jesus is teaching us to go the second mile. That means taking the kind of action that will turn those lemons into lemonade.

Transition

Now, what would happen if you applied this verse to your marriage that has gone a little, or a lot sour? What if you applied this verse to personal problems that are unresolved? What if you applied this verse to work, to your profession, or to your schooling? Indeed, what kind of church would this church be if every member was a second mile Christian?

F. Visualization of the Solution

Let me give you an example of what could happen. A church member called, asking if she might bring by a neighbor who was divorcing her husband. The family had three small children. I agreed to see the neighbor.

The member brought the woman to my study, introduced her and then left the study.

The woman looked across the desk at me and said, "I am of another faith. I am here because I'm a good friend with your church member. She asked me to come, thinking it might help. My husband is an alcoholic and a workaholic. I want away from him. Nothing you can say will stop the divorce."

"It sounds like your husband needs help," I replied. "When you talk to him again, will you suggest that he also come to see me? Perhaps, I can help him."

She agreed saying, "He really does need help."

A few days later, he called and we set up an appointment. He came in promptly. He was in his thirties and had a responsible position with a large oil company. He sat down across from me.

I looked at him and said, "Your wife says she is divorcing you because you are an alcoholic and a workaholic."

He replied, "That's about right."

I asked him, "What do you want?"

"I want my wife back," he replied. "I want my children back. I want my home back."

"There's a chance that could happen," I said to him. "But it would mean that you must stop drinking immediately. It would mean that you must become the man your wife can love again. It may take a long time. There may be disappointments. Are you willing to try?"

"I'm willing to do whatever it takes," he said.

Then I said, "You're going to need more help than I can give you. You will need the help of your Heavenly Father."

"Will you bow with me in prayer?" I asked. "Will you ask the Lord to forgive you for the mess you have made of your life and marriage? Will you ask him to help you to never take another drink?"

"Will you ask him to help you become the man your wife can love? Will you ask him to help you to never, never give up?" I added.

He said quietly, "I'm ready to do it right now."

We knelt in prayer. He poured out his heart to the Lord, and asked for God's help. After we had prayed, we agreed to meet on a regular basis. I explained to him that he must help his wife with the divorce. That he must be faithful in her support. That he must be prompt in picking up and returning the children on days of visitation.

I explained that he must be kind and helpful: that he must not be confrontational, or angry.

"In other words, you must be a Christian gentleman. That is the man your wife may love again," I said in conclusion.

Months went by. He stayed sober and he stayed faithful to his commitment to try to win his family back. Then one day he sat across from me with a big smile on his face.

"What are you grinning about?" I asked.

"You won't believe what happened this past weekend," he said. "I picked up the children promptly as I always do, on my day to have them."

He continued, "We had a good day and I brought them back promptly, as I always do. When I brought them to the door, you won't believe what my wife said."

"What did she say?" I asked, relishing his obvious pleasure in talking about it.

She asked, "Would you like to come in and help me put the children to bed?"

"I would love to," I replied. "We bathed the children and put them in their pajamas, and tucked them in bed."

He stopped and grinned at me again. "Do you know what she did then? She asked me if I would like to have a cup of coffee."

"We sat by the fire and talked into the evening," he said. "I thanked her for the evening and told her it had been one of the very best days I had had in many months. And then I left."

He looked at me and asked, "Do you think I handled it right?"

I grinned back at him and said, "I think you handled it just right."

What I could have said was, "Man, you've been making lemonade!" But he wouldn't have understood the remark.

A day or two later my phone rang. It was the wife. It was the first time I had spoken to her since she left my office determined to divorce her husband.

"I can't believe I'm saying this," she said. Her voice was husky with feeling. "Pastor, I want my husband back. How do I go about getting him back?"

I smiled into the phone and said, "You have just gone beyond my expertise. But you don't need my help in that regard. You know how to get your husband back, don't you?"

"Yes, of course," she answered. "That's my part isn't it? And I can do it."

Then I said, "When the two of you have reconciled, please come to see me. We'll ask God to help both of you to make a fresh start; to let the old things pass away. We'll ask God to make your marriage new and lasting."

That is exactly what they did. Not long after that they were transferred to another state. I didn't see them for several years. Then they turned up at a wedding I was performing. They were obviously very much in love.

Sermon Conclusion

Sermon Summary

That husband acted on the principle of the second mile. He took a bunch of lemons that he rightly deserved and turned them into lemonade. He took what seemed to be a lost situation and applied the spirit of the second mile. He showed his wife a face of humility and kindness. He made any sacrifice to win back his family. He continued to hope and love, even when it was hard to love. Most importantly, he asked for grace and strength from the Lord to help him save his family from the blight of divorce.

Transition

What are the lemons in your life? What are you going to do about them? Are you going to just sit there and suck on them until your face screws up into a pucker of perpetual unhappiness? Isn't it time to go the second mile?

G. Call for Response

Jesus is teaching us to take the lemons of life and make lemonade. He is teaching us to take action.

He is calling on us to apply the principle of the second mile. He is asking us to go the second mile in kindness, patience, forgiveness and effort.

H. Invitation

Invitation to Christians

I have highlighted Matthew 5:41 in these two Bibles. I am going to place one on each side of the platform. I want to invite you to come forward and touch the highlighted verse. In that act you will be saying, "Lord, I need your help. I want to be a second mile Christian. Please forgive me where I have failed. Give me the strength to do this."

Would you say this as a prayer right now? Would you pray, "Lord, help me to be a second mile Christian"? Now, mean it, and on the invitation come and touch Matthew 5:41. Then find a place here at the altar to talk to the Lord. Ask for his help. Make your commitment now.

Invitation to Faith and Baptism

Friends, while church members are coming to touch the Bibles, I want to ask you a question. Aren't you thankful that Jesus went the second mile? He went to the cross to die for your sins and mine. There are lemons in your life. He is here today to help you. He wants to help you turn your life around.

43

I will be here at the front to assist you as you make your decision. Come up and shake my hand. Let it be a sign that today you are putting your trust in Jesus Christ.

He will forgive you of your sins. He will enter your life and become your Savior. And, some day, he will take you to heaven.

Come now. We will arrange for your baptism and membership in this good church.

Invitation to Membership

And dear friends, you may want to join this good church today by transfer of your church membership. We will joyfully receive you and assist you.

I. Afterglow

And now may the peace of God, which passes all understanding, keep your hearts and minds through Christ Jesus. Amen.

Chapter 6
Expository Sermon in the Persuasive Form

Ministers who major on expository preaching will typically develop a series of sermons on a book of the Bible, or on a large section of scripture such as the Sermon on the Mount. However, any sermon may be considered expository if the text is explained and the scriptural truths are the focus of the message.

An expository sermon explains or uncovers the meaning of a passage of scripture. First, the sermon or teaching explains what the passage meant to those who first received it. Second, the sermon or teaching explains the relevance of the passage to the present audience.

Many expository sermons have a persuasive goal. This is true because the Holy Scriptures, especially the New Testament, were written to be transformative in individual lives. Jesus came to seek and to save that which was lost.

Form follows Function

Nature teaches us that form follows function, or that the shape of a thing is determined by its purpose or function. Examples are all around us. Fish are designed to breathe underwater. Birds have feathers that facilitate flying.

The field of architecture is an example of form follows function. Hospitals and service stations are very different facilities because they have different purposes or functions. Form follows function. This principle applies to preaching.

Expository sermon content that is persuasive will be more effective when it is written in a persuasive sermon form.

The Persuasive Expository Sermon

Typically, a persuasive sermon comes into being when the minister finds a need or problem that is being addressed by a portion of scripture. An expository sermon that is meant to be persuasive will always be about the resolution of a problem or need.

It could also be that the minister has searched the Bible to find a scripture passage that speaks to a particular human problem, current event, church need, or social concern. The persuasive sermon grows out of a study of the biblical passage.

The minister then engages in several steps to create a sermon abstract for the persuasive sermon. The sermon abstract is the blueprint that guides the sermon building process.

Create the Sermon Abstract

Step One: Uncover problem or need that will become the focus of the persuasive sermon.

Step Two: Select the scripture text that will address the problem or need. The problem or need may have been discovered in a portion of scripture that was under study, or the text may have been specifically selected because it deals with the problem or need.

Step Three: Perform an exegetical study of the scripture passage. This distills the biblical truths that will be applied to resolve the problem or need.

Asking and answering the following questions about the scripture passage of the sermon will be helpful in creating the sermon abstract. The resultant study notes will also be valuable in building the sermon.

1. Who wrote it?

2. When was it written?

3. Who was the intended audience?

4. What was the writer's purpose?

5. What is the larger context?

6. What is the essential meaning of words and phrases used?

7. What light do other scriptures shed on its meaning?

8. What do other preachers and commentators say about the passage?

9. After thorough study, what is your conclusive understanding of it?

Step Four: Prepare the sermon abstract.

1. List the central truths of the selected passage.

2. Write a statement that clearly defines the problem or need to be resolved.

3. Use the central truth or truths of the scripture passage to write a statement that will explain the scriptural solution to the problem or need.

4. Write a purpose statement that explains the goal of the sermon.

Write the Persuasive Expository Sermon

Use the sermon abstract as a blueprint to write the persuasive sermon, utilizing the nine steps of the persuasive sermon form.

1. Refine the statement that explains the need or problem that will be presented to the audience.

2. Refine the statement that explains the scriptural solution to be presented to the listeners.

3. Refine the purpose statement that explains the response that will be asked of the audience.

4. Determine how you will help the audience visualize the scriptural solution.

5. Determine how the call for response and invitation will be presented to accomplish the sermon purpose.

6. Add scriptures, illustrations, quotes, statistics, etc., to the sermon points as needed.

7. Determine what (if any) follow up there will be to the sermon.

8. Then complete the three steps of the sermon introduction. Give special consideration to how your sermon will transition from the "Attention" step to the "Body of the Sermon."

9. Make use of sermon prompts. These are the signs along the sermon path that guide from point to point. I have found that words such as transition, review, summary, application, illustration, question, humor, quote, etc. are helpful.

10. Write an appropriate afterglow to conclude the sermon time.

11. If possible, record and listen to the message. Critique and refine it.

The Model Expository Sermon

The model expository sermon in Chapter Seven will visualize the persuasive sermon form. It demonstrates how the scripture text is applied to resolve the problem or need presented to the congregation, i.e., the insight to be gained from the sermon.

The model sermon was adapted and presented to an audience of about 300 at Woodland Acres Baptist Church, Tulsa, Oklahoma. The sermon was part of a Sunday morning communion service. The service concluded with a silent invitation (decision cards) rather than an altar call.

Those attending were asked to respond to the service by completing decision cards. These cards were to be placed in the offering plates at the conclusion of the service.

I was overjoyed by what the decision cards revealed. Eleven people joined the Woodland Acres Baptist Church by membership transfer that morning. There were three confessions of faith. Scores of others expressed love and devotion to the Savior who died for them.

Chapter 7
Model Expository Sermon

Sermon Abstract

Title: How can we be rescued?

Scripture: Romans 5:6-11

Central Truths of the Passage

God's word reveals that we're unsaved and in need of God's grace. We're ungodly and sinful. We are at enmity with God, and under the wrath of God. We're without strength and can't save ourselves.

Because God loves us he has sent us a Savior who is Christ the Lord. Jesus has given his own sinless body and blood to redeem us. He can save us from our sins and deliver us from God's wrath.

Problem/Need to be Resolved

We're adrift in a world of sin. We're without hope, condemned and under the wrath of God.

Biblical Solution to the Problem/Need

Jesus Christ is God's gift of love. He came to redeem us from eternal death. He wants to forgive us and to give us the gift of everlasting life.

Sermon Purpose

To invite men, women, youths and children, to call upon the Lord for salvation

Introduction to the Sermon

A. Goodwill

Good morning. I'm so happy to see you in church this Lord's Day. I believe God has given me a wonderful word to share with you.

B. Pre-Invitation

There will be an invitation at the conclusion of the message this morning. I will step down to the front of the sanctuary to welcome and assist those of you who desire to unite with this church by transfer of membership.

Some may want to use this occasion to make a public confession of faith in our Lord Jesus Christ. We will receive you joyfully and arrange for your baptism.

Now, I know that there are many reasons why we are here today. God has promised to be among us. Would each of you be open to hear His voice? Thank you.

Transition: Please turn to Romans 5:6-11

C. Attention

Illustration

Ice fishing is a favorite sport up north. I read a story of 135 fishermen who ventured out on the ice flow of Lake Erie. They became trapped when the ice broke away from the shoreline. One poor man fell into the water and later died of a heart attack.

The Coast Guard came to the rescue. Some of the fishermen were airlifted by helicopter. Some were taken to shore by air boats.

I was interested in what one of the fishermen said. He said, "We were in no danger. We knew there was enough ice out there."

To which I say, "If that's true, then why aren't you still out there fishing?"

Some of you may be thinking, "Why did the pastor tell us that bit of news?" Here's the reason.

Body of the Sermon

D. Problem-Need to be Resolved

Those fishermen are an analogy of our own human situation. We're adrift: not in an icy lake, but in a sea of sin. Some of us sense the danger. Some are oblivious to it. But we all need rescue. As we read today's scripture passage it will become clear why we all need to be rescued.

Read Scripture Passage, Romans 5:6-11:

6 For when we were yet without strength, in due time Christ died for the ungodly.

7 For scarcely for a righteous man will one die: yet peradventure for a good man some would even dare to die.

8 But God commended his love toward us, in that, while we were yet sinners, Christ died for us.

9 Much more then, being now justified by his blood, we shall be saved from wrath through him.

10 For if, when we were enemies, we were reconciled to God by the death of his Son, much more, being reconciled, we shall be saved by his life.

11 And not only so, but we also joy in God through our Lord Jesus Christ, by whom we have now received the atonement. (KJV)

Question

What does this passage teach us about the dangers of being without Christ? How does it describe those who are unsaved, i.e., those who have never put their trust in the Lord?

Exposition:

1. We're without strength and ungodly. (6)

2. We're sinners. (8)

3. We're objects of God's wrath. (9)

4. We're enemies of God and not saved. (10)

5. We're separated from God. (11)

Discuss the Implications of these Truths:

The Bible clearly teaches that we have no strength to save ourselves. When the scriptures describe the unsaved as ungodly, it means that we are without God and opposed to God and his will for this world. We are dead in sins and trespasses. God's judgment already rests on us.

What does it mean to be without Christ in this world? The Bible clearly states that it means we are doomed to an eternity of darkness; a darkness of remorse and separation from all that is good and godly.

Can we be rescued? Yes. That's the good news of this passage.

E. Solution to the Problem/Need

Explain the Scripture Passage

1. God the Father sent his son Jesus Christ, to save us (6).

2. Jesus sacrificed his sinless body and blood to redeem us at a time when humanity was in rebellion against the Lord (6).

3. God sent his Son to save us because he loves us (7-8).

4. The blood of Christ covers the multitude of our sins and justifies us in the eyes of God. Jesus delivers us from God's wrath when we believe and accept his sacrifice for us (9).

5. Jesus' death saves us from death and hell, and gives us eternal life and heaven (10).

6. Jesus is the means whereby we who were the enemies of God can become the friends of God (11).

Transition

Our time together began with a story. It was the story of a group of ice fisherman trapped on an ice flow in Lake Erie. That story was used as an analogy of our own world trapped in a sea of sin. God's word has taught us we can be rescued. We can be saved.

F. Visualization of the Solution

Let me close by telling you a story that illustrates what can happen when we trust in the Lord.

Illustration

It's the story of another group of people literally trapped in ice and water. It was the night of April 14, 1912. The RMS Titanic was on its maiden voyage.

On board was a 39-year-old minister with his 6-year-old daughter. There was no mother because she had died. John Harper was on his way to the United States to preach at the great Moody Church of Chicago for a period of three months.

The Titanic rammed an iceberg in the North Atlantic. The unsinkable Titanic began to sink. Harper got his daughter into a lifeboat. Then he went back and began to comfort the passengers by sharing with them the hope of Christ. More than 1500 souls went into the icy water. Only six of those would be pulled into life boats. A young man floating on debris was one of them.

The rest we know from a survivors meeting some four years afterward. That same young man rose to speak. The young man testified, "I was John Harper's last convert to Christ."

He told how he floated on the debris without a life jacket. He said Harper swam over to him and asked, "Are you saved?"

The young man said, "No." Harper sought to persuade him to believe, but the young man, near shock, again said, "No."

John Harper then took off his life jacket and threw it to the man and said, "Here then, you need this more than I do," and swam away to other people.

A few minutes later Harper swam back to the young man and succeeded in leading him to salvation.

Harper tried to swim away to help others but the cold had sapped his strength. Just before he slipped beneath the waves he called out to any who might hear, "Believe on the name of the Lord Jesus and you will be saved."

Then he was gone.

Conclusion to the Sermon

Sermon Summary

What has God's word taught us this morning? God's word reveals that we who inhabit this world are unsaved. We are ungodly and sinful. We're at enmity with God and under the wrath of God. We're without strength and cannot save ourselves.

Because of God's love for us he has sent us a Savior who is Christ the Lord. Jesus has given his own sinless body and blood to redeem us. He can save us from our sins and deliver us from God's wrath.

G. Call for Response

Someday the Lord will return. The age of grace will come to an end. The judgment of the world will begin. But for now, Christ is waiting with open arms to receive those who will come to him. He is calling to you. I believe this is God's time for you.

H. Invitation

Invitation to Faith and Baptism

Please bow in prayer. Please, no one should be looking around, not even the youngest child. Thank you. Now if you are here this morning and you are not saved, if you are not a Christian yet, will you simply lift your head and look at me. Thank you.

I want to tell you what John Harper told the dark night. I want to tell you what he told the icy Atlantic. I want to tell you what he told any who could hear his voice, "Believe on the name of the Lord Jesus and you will be saved."

Please bow your heads again in prayer. I am going to pray a prayer of faith. Anyone here this morning may pray it with me quietly in your heart. Or, you may listen to the prayer. Then, if the prayer says what you want to say to God this morning, then you can pray, "Lord, that's my prayer."

Prayer: Please repeat this prayer quietly now in your heart. "Lord Jesus, be merciful to me. I am one of those you died on the cross to save. I repent of my sins, and trust you now and forever with my eternal soul. Amen."

Question

Did you mean that prayer? Then, come now and give me your hand as a sign that you will trust the Lord to be your Savior today, tomorrow and forever. Come now.

Now let us all stand and sing. I will be waiting for you so that I may welcome you into the family of God, and into the fellowship of this church.

Invitation to Church Membership

The invitation is extended to include Christian guests who may desire to worship and serve God as a member of this good church. I'm here to welcome and assist you in your decision. Please come now.

I. Afterglow

But let all take refuge in you and be glad. Let them ever sing for joy. Spread your protection over us; that those who love your name may rejoice in you.
Psalm 5:11

Chapter 8
Narrative Sermon in the Persuasive Form

The Bible is filled with religious history, unique stories, and interesting characters. The purpose of this chapter is to help ministers to use this rich reservoir to write narrative sermons in the persuasive sermon form.

The narrative sermon can be an effective tool to make Bible history, stories and characters come alive for the listener. A narrative sermon may be remembered long after it was preached. That is the nature of a story on the human mind.

Value of Biblical Narratives

From early church history to the present time, the story of the Christian faith has been taught through stories drawn from the Old and New Testament.

The various strains of the modern Christian faith are held together like a patchwork quilt by the commonality of our stories. Whatever our denominational badge, we celebrate Christmas and the story of the birth of the Christ Child. Whatever our denominational doctrine, we celebrate Easter and the story of the risen Christ.

Value of Narrative Preaching

Narrative preaching can touch human lives with God. Life-changing decisions can occur for those who hear and identify with Bible narratives. That is the purpose of narrative sermons in the persuasive sermon form.

We humans love stories. Our minds are geared to follow a story from beginning to end. And the story has staying power with the listener.

The narrative sermon stretches the speaker's gift of preaching more than any other sermon genre. Narrative sermons may deal with a wide range of human emotions. There may be moments of drama, moments of humor, and moments of wonder as the story unfolds. And there is always the point of the story, which is the application of the truth contained in the narrative.

Narrative sermons are some of the most effective persuasive sermons in accomplishing the sermon purpose.

These sermon purposes nay include reaching the unsaved, reviving the angry and bitter, healing the broken-hearted, energizing the discouraged, and lifting up those caught in the throes of hopelessness.

The Narrative Sermon in the Persuasive Form

The persuasive narrative sermon has three main sections: introduction, body and conclusion. Each main section has three subsections for a total of nine. These are identified by the letters A through I, and correspond to the nine steps of the persuasive sermon form explained in Chapter Two.

Introduction to the Sermon

The introduction precedes and sets the stage for the story of the narrative sermon. It contains three subdivisions: goodwill, pre-invitation and attention.

A. Goodwill

The minister creates an atmosphere of friendliness and acceptance for the narrative sermon.

B. Pre-Invitation

The minister informs the audience that the narrative sermon will conclude with an invitation to faith in Christ and Church membership. This removes the uncertainty about the conclusion of the sermon and permits the listener time to contemplate a response.

C. Attention

The minister uses this step to secure the interest of the listener for the story portion of the narrative sermon.

An analogy would be the information printed on the inside or back cover of a book. It's written to be so interesting that the reader will buy the book.

Body of the Sermon

The body of the persuasive narrative sermon is the narrative story. The story contains three subdivisions: problem or need, biblical solution and visualization.

D. Problem or Need to be Resolved

The minister shows the audience that a problem or need exists. He explains that the problem or need is addressed in the narrative story that is the text for the sermon. And just as in the narrative story, the present day problem or need should be resolved.

E. The Solution to the Problem or Need

The minister explains how the problem or need was resolved within the narrative story, and then helps the audience to see that the scriptural solution can be effective in resolving the present-day problem or need.

F. The Visualization of the Solution

The minister explains to the listeners what happened when the solution was applied within the narrative story, and then demonstrates what could happen if the biblical solution is applied to the present day problem or need.

Conclusion to the Sermon

There are three sub-divisions to the conclusion of the narrative sermon: call for response, invitation, and afterglow.

The minister makes concluding comments about the narrative story of the sermon and summarizes the sermon.

G. The Call for Response

The minister then explains how he believes God would have the listeners to respond to the narrative sermon.

H. The Invitation

The invitation offered by the minister is consistent with the sermon purpose.

Invitation to the Target Audience

The invitation calls on the listener to adopt the biblical solution of the sermon. The minister may do this by inviting listeners to come to the altar. He might ask them to stand at their seats in decision. He may ask them to complete a decision card and to bring it to the altar, or return it in the offering plate. The sermon purpose will influence the kind of invitation that's planned for the sermon completion.

The minister should also think beyond the altar call. Perhaps the minister has asked the listener to commit to a program of witnessing. A follow-up might include a training event and regular participation in church outreach. Those who have made decisions could be contacted and enrolled in the planned emphasis.

When the primary purpose of the sermon has been accomplished the minister then presents the post-invitation appeal to faith in Christ and church membership. This action concludes the invitation.

Invitation to Faith and Baptism

Invitation to Church Membership

I. Afterglow

The minister closes the service with brief and appropriate words that signal to the congregation his warm regard for them. He may pray for them or bless them to conclude his part in the service.

Writing a Persuasive Narrative Sermon

The minister selects and studies the scriptural story-narrative that is to be the basis for the narrative sermon.

Prepare the Sermon Abstract

Step One: Write a statement of the problem or need in the narrative story.

Step Two: Write a statement of the solution to the problem or need in the story.

Step Three: Write a statement explaining how the biblical solution that is utilized in the story can be used to resolve a similar need or problem that exists in present time.

Step Four: Write a purpose statement explaining how the listener will be asked to respond to the solution.

After the sermon abstract has been completed, the minister uses it as a blueprint for building the narrative sermon in the PSF.

Write the Persuasive Sermon

1. Refine the statement that explains the need or problem that will be presented to the audience.

2. Refine the statement that explains the scriptural solution to be presented to the listeners.

3. Refine the statement that explains the response that will be asked of the audience.

4. Determine how you will help the audience visualize the scriptural solution.

5. Determine how the call for response and invitation will be presented to accomplish the sermon purpose.

6. Add scriptures, illustrations, quotes, statistics, etc., to the sermon points as needed.

7. Determine what (if any) follow up there will be to the sermon.

8. Then complete the three steps of the sermon introduction. Give special consideration to how your sermon will transition from the "Attention" step to the "Body of the Sermon."

9. Make use of sermon prompts.

10. Write the appropriate afterglow to conclude the sermon time.

11. If possible, record and listen to the message. Critique and refine it.

Model Narrative Sermon

Chapter Nine contains a model narrative sermon in the nine steps of the persuasive sermon form. Please note how the scriptural solution that is within the story becomes the basis for the call to action.

This sermon has been used five times in the past five years. The congregations to whom it was presented all favorably received it and responded to it. It seemed to be especially helpful to those who were facing an important decision or a personal crisis.

Chapter 9
Model Narrative Sermon

Sermon Abstract

Title: How can I face personal crises God's way?

Scripture: 2 Samuel 15:13-14, 26

13 And there came a messenger to David, saying, the hearts of the men of Israel are after Absalom.

14 And David said to all his servants that were with him at Jerusalem, Arise, and let us flee; for we shall not else escape from Absalom: make speed to depart, lest he overtake us suddenly, and bring evil upon us, and smite the city with the edge of the sword.

26 But if he thus says, I have no delight in you; behold, here am I, let him do to me as seems good to him.

Central Truths in the Story

King David faced the loss of his kingdom and life. His whole family was in jeopardy. His conduct in the face of this crisis gives us clues into how God would have us deal with personal crises.

13. Awareness: David learned the facts of the crisis.

14. Assessment: David honestly assessed the danger facing him in the crisis.

14. Action: David selected a course of action to meet the crisis.

14. Accountability: David considered the consequences of his action on others.

26. Allegiance: David trusted God for the outcome.

Problem/Need to be Resolved

Absalom led a rebellion against his father, King David. It threatened David's life, family and kingdom.

Biblical Solution to the Problem/Need

David took five steps to meet his personal crisis: awareness, assessment, action, accountability and allegiance.

Sermon Purpose

To encourage listeners to meet life's personal crises through the five steps followed by King David

Introduction to the Sermon

A. Goodwill

I'm so glad to see you this morning. I'm acutely aware of the significance of this weekend. It's another anniversary of 9-11. God has laid a special message on my heart to share with you.

B. Pre-Invitation

There will be an invitation at the conclusion of the message this morning. I will step down to the front of the sanctuary to welcome and assist those of you who desire to unite with this church by transfer of membership.

Some may want to use this occasion to make a public confession of faith in our Lord Jesus Christ. We will receive you joyfully and arrange for your baptism.

Now, I know that there are many reasons why we are here today. God has promised to be among us. Would each of you be open to hear His voice? Thank you.

C. Attention

September 11, 2001, is an anniversary of national crisis. It's also an anniversary of death for almost three thousand souls who perished in the twin towers, the Pentagon, and the four passenger planes that were crashed.

It's also an anniversary of personal crisis for the thousands of loved ones and friends of those who perished.

This morning we're going to talk about handling personal crisis.

Question

What is the definition of a personal crisis? A crisis is a crucial or decisive point or situation; a turning point. It's an emotionally stressful event or traumatic change in a person's life.

Question

What would constitute a crisis in your life? Some would say facing a life-threatening or debilitating disease. Some might say experiencing great financial reversals. Would the death of a loved one be a crisis? Yes, of course. Might marriage or family problems constitute a crisis?

Transition

Our scripture study this morning is about King David of the Old Testament. David found God's way of handling a life crisis that could have cost him his kingdom and his life. In this story I believe God gives us valuable clues for dealing with personal crises.

Body of the Sermon

Discuss the background events that led to King David's crisis

By the time of King David's reign, Israel had lost the concept of marriage as a relationship between one man and one woman.

Further, David was corrupted by following the example of despotic kings who had many wives and concubines. David felt at liberty to take another man's wife.

He called Bathsheba to him and had his way with her. The result was a pregnancy.

Rather than confess and repent of the terrible thing he had done; David compounded his sin by having Uriah, Bathsheba's husband, killed in battle. He thought he had hidden his sin.

Nathan, God's prophet, exposed the evil that the king had committed. Then with his horrible behavior exposed, David repented and sought God's forgiveness. The Lord graciously forgave him.

But David had sown to the wind and he would reap the whirlwind. David was faced with one crisis after another.

The infant born to Bathsheba died.

Amnon, David's son, raped his half-sister Tamar.

Two years later, Absalom, Tamar's brother, had Amnon murdered.

Absalom fled from King David. He was estranged from his father for three years. David finally allowed his return but didn't see him for an additional two years. Then they were seemingly reconciled.

However, Absalom was angry with his father and plotted the overthrow of the kingdom. Absalom rallied a large number of the people to his cause. He went to Hebron (where the Tribe of Judah had crowned David king) and mounted a revolt against King David.

D. Problem/Need to be Resolved

As we shall see from the scripture study, David faced the loss of his kingdom and life. His whole family was in jeopardy. Failure to meet and manage this crisis would cost him everything.

His conduct in the face of this crisis offers us clues into how God would have us deal with personal crises. It may be a crisis some are facing at this very moment. Or, it may be a crisis that is coming.

Read and explain the scripture passage: 2 Samuel 15:13-14, 26

13 And there came a messenger to David, saying, the hearts of the men of Israel are after Absalom.

14 And David said to all his servants that were with him at Jerusalem, Arise, and let us flee; for we shall not else escape from Absalom: make speed to depart, lest he overtake us suddenly, and bring evil upon us, and smite the city with the edge of the sword.

26 But if he thus says, I have no delight in you; behold, here am I, let him do to me as seems good to him. (KJV)

E. Biblical Solution to the Problem/Need

God's solution for David's personal crisis seemed to have five steps. They're revealed in the conduct of David in meeting this crisis which threatened his life, his family, and his kingdom.

1. Awareness (13): David learned the facts of the crisis facing him.

2. Assessment (14): David honestly assessed the danger facing him in the crisis.

3. Action (14): David selected a course of action to meet the crisis.

4. Accountability (14): David considered others in the actions he would take.

5. Allegiance (26): David trusted God for the outcome of the crisis.

Question

What was the outcome of David's actions to meet this crisis? David used his wisdom and experience to gain time. Then he organized his forces and defeated Absalom. In the process Absalom was killed. The heart of David was broken by the death of this rebellious son. His grief seemed unbearable.

Yet, King David did what we all must do after the passing of a personal crisis. He picked up the pieces of his life and went on.

Read: 2 Samuel 19:7-8a

> *7 Now therefore arise, go forth, and speak comfortably unto thy servants: for I swear by the LORD, if you go not forth, there will not tarry one with you this night: and that will be worse to you than all the evil that befell you from your youth until now.*
>
> *8 Then the king arose, and sat in the gate. And they told to all the people, saying, Behold, the king sits in the gate. And all*

the people came before the king: for Israel had fled every man to his tent.

Transition

As we come to the close of our time together I want to tell you the story of one man who faced his own personal crisis on 9/11. I believe he exemplified how God might have us deal with the crisis we are facing now, or will face in the future. His name was Todd Beamer.

F. Visualization of the Solution

Todd and Lisa Beamer were Christians. They taught Sunday school in their church. Todd was pursuing a successful business career.

He boarded United Flight 93 on September 11, 2001, on his way to a business meeting in California. The flight was hijacked by terrorists. The terrorists were apparently intent on crashing the plane into a target in Washington, D.C.

Todd used an inboard telephone and contacted telephone operator Lisa Jefferson. Lisa informed him that other planes had been hijacked and that the planes had been crashed into targets.

During their approximately 13 minutes of conversation, Beamer told the operator that he and other passengers were going to try to overcome the terrorists. He asked her to pray with him and together they recited the 23rd Psalm:

The Lord is my shepherd; I shall not want. He makes me to lie down in green pastures. He leads me beside the still waters. He restores my soul. He leads me in the paths of righteousness for His name's sake.

*Yes, though I walk through the valley of the shadow of death
I will fear no evil, for You are with me. Your rod and Your
staff, they comfort me. You prepare a table before me in the
presence of my enemies. You anoint my head with oil. My cup
runs over.*

*Surely goodness and mercy shall follow me all the days of my
life, and I will dwell in the house of the Lord forever. Amen.*

He asked the operator to promise him that she would call his
pregnant wife and two sons. Then he dropped the phone. The
line was still open.

The last words the operator heard were these: "Let's roll."

Flight 93 never became a terrorist missile to be crashed into
the Capitol or the White House. It went down in a field in
Pennsylvania, taking the lives of all on board. We can only
surmise that the passengers charged the cockpit and stopped the
terrorist mission of flight 93.

Conclusion to the Sermon

Sermon Summary

I believe I can see Todd Beamer using the same solution as did
King David to meet this crisis.

1. Awareness: He became aware of the crisis.

2. Assessment: He honestly assessed the facts of the crisis.

3. Action: He chose a course of action and followed it.

4. Accountability: He carefully considered the consequences of
his action on others.

5. Allegiance: He prayed about his actions and trusted God for
the outcome.

The two stories have very different outcomes. Todd Beamer died as a young man, giving his life to save the lives of others. King David continued to rule Israel. He died at the age of 70, one of the greatest figures of history.

G. Call for Response

How would God have us respond to the stories of King David and Todd Beamer this morning?

We can do what they did. We can take our personal crisis to the Lord. We can ask him to help us follow the steps that will meet our crisis.

H. Invitation

Invitation to the Target Audience

I invite you to find a place here at the altar. You may stand, sit, or kneel. Talk to the Lord about what's facing you. Commit yourself and your crisis to him. Trust him for the outcome, and then take the action he has impressed on your heart.

Invitation to Membership

Christian friend, while people are coming to pray, I want to invite you to join this good church. We will welcome and assist you.

Invitation to Faith and Baptism

Friends, we all need the Lord to face the personal crises of life. This would be a wonderful Sunday to begin the Christian journey. We will joyfully receive you and this good church will arrange for your baptism.

I. Afterglow

Ask the congregation to join you in repeating Psalm 23.

SECTION TWO

Ten Persuasive Sermons

For

Special Days

Chapter 10
Sermon for the New Year

Sermon Abstract

Title: How can I make this year a success?

Scripture: Joshua 14:10-12

Central Truth of the Scripture Passage

The Old Testament figure of Caleb is a model for us on how to keep our faith and triumph over adversity.

Problem/Need to be Resolved

The New Year is a time to make resolutions and a fresh start. However, many people feel overwhelmed by life's problems.

They are reluctant to even hope for something better. They feel too old, or too tired, or too defeated, to expect the New Year to be any different.

Biblical Solution to the Problem/Need

There are four characteristics in the life of the Old Testament character Caleb that offer us a wonderful hope for victory over life's obstacles in the New Year.

Caleb was a man of vision, virtue, vigor, and victories.

Sermon Purpose

To lead the listeners to commit to the four characteristics of Caleb that lead to victory over life's obstacles

Introduction to the Sermon

A. Goodwill

It is so good to see you on the first Sunday of a New Year. I think attending church on the first Sunday of a New Year is about the best possible way to get the year off to a good start. Do you agree? Turn to your neighbor, smile and wish them a Happy New Year. Do it now.

How are you doing with your New Year's resolutions? Did I hear a groan? Have you already given up on the New Year? Then, I have a good word for you. I believe it's possible to make this one of the best years of your life.

Transition: Please turn to Joshua 14:10-12

B. Pre-Invitation

There will be an invitation at the conclusion of the message this morning. I will step down to the front of the sanctuary to welcome and assist those of you who desire to unite with this church by transfer of membership.

Some may want to use the first Sunday of this New Year to make a public confession of faith in our Lord Jesus Christ. We will receive you joyfully and arrange for your baptism.

Now I know that there are many reasons why we are here today. God has promised to be among us. Would each of you be open to hear His voice? Thank you.

C. Attention

There are 365 days, 8,760 hours, 525,600 minutes, 31,536,000 seconds in this year.

What are you planning to achieve with the 31 million heartbeats of this New Year? Will you achieve all of your goals?

Isn't there something that you haven't achieved that you still want to achieve? Isn't there an old habit you want to break? Isn't there a skill you want to acquire? Isn't there a mountain you want to climb?

Body of the Sermon

D. Problem/Need to be Resolved

"Yes," you say. "But pastor, I've tried making resolutions and setting goals. Then I fail and my hopes and dreams are often crushed. I'm too old. I'm too tired. I'm just too defeated to expect this year to be any different."

E. Biblical Solution to the Problem/Need

This year can be different. Have you considered Caleb? The Old Testament story of Caleb offers us a wonderful hope. It's the hope that, like Caleb, we can overcome life's obstacles and meet new challenges.

Read Scripture: Joshua 14:10-12

> *10 And now, behold, the Lord hath kept me alive, as he said, these forty and five years, even since the Lord spoke this word to Moses, while the children of Israel wandered in the wilderness: and now, lo, I am this day 85 years old.*
>
> *11 As yet I am as strong this day as I was in the day that Moses sent me: as my strength was then, even so is my strength now, for war, both to go out, and to come in.*
>
> *12 Now therefore give me this mountain, whereof the Lord spoke in that day; for you heard in that day how the Anakims*

were there, and that the cities were great and fenced: if so be
the Lord will be with me, then I shall be able to drive them
out, as the Lord said.

Explain the Scripture Passage

Look back 45 years from the time of this passage to that time
when the Israelites first came to the borders of Canaan. They
sent out 12 spies to explore the land. Caleb was one of them.

They reported back that the land was a good land. But ten of
the spies said there was no way it could be taken because the
cities were walled; and the walls were defended by great
warriors.

Two voices dissented. They were the voices of Joshua and
Caleb.

Both said that God would give the land into the hands of
Israel if Israel had the courage to seize it.

You know what happened. The people quaked with fear and
went back into the wilderness. They wandered until that whole
adult generation died. The only exceptions were Joshua and
Caleb.

Transition

Now, 45 years later we have this stirring speech by Caleb. What
does this 85 year-old warrior say? Caleb said, "Give me this
mountain."

Caleb is talking about Mount Hebron. The mount is located
19 miles south of Jerusalem. It is a 3000 foot plateau. There is
abundant water. It has good land.

Now listen to this. It's also the burial place of Abraham,
Sarah, Isaac, Rebecca, Jacob and Leah. It's holy ground.

E. Biblical Solution Continued

Caleb had 4 characteristics that we can adopt that will help us finish this New Year the way God intends.

1. First, Caleb was a man of vision.

All of the spies saw things as they were. But only Joshua and Caleb saw things as they could be.

Yes, Caleb saw things as they were. But he also saw a home for the people of God. He saw a good land that was well adapted to their needs. He saw a permanent place of worship.

Application

Just now, look at your life. What do you see? Be honest: see things as they are. Now look again. Can you see your life as God intends it to be? If so, then you are becoming a Caleb. You are becoming a person of vision!

All of us need direction. But it must be the right direction. That is what God wants to give us this morning.

2. Second, Caleb was a man of virtue.

We know this because the Bible says he wholly followed the Lord. **Look at Joshua 14:8**

Nevertheless my brethren that went up with me made the heart of the people melt: but I wholly followed the Lord my God.

Please understand. The Bible is not saying Caleb was perfect. If Caleb was perfect then none of us can follow his example. The Bible is saying that Caleb knew what he believed, and who he believed.

The Bible is saying Caleb was persistent. He followed the Lord through 40 years of frustration in the desert.

Illustration

I'm reminded of John Newton, the author of the hymn, "Amazing Grace." Newton was old and nearly blind, yet he still preached on. He became so feeble that he had to have someone stand with him in the pulpit.

Once he spoke in a voice that was barely a whisper saying, "Jesus is so precious."

Then he said it again, "Jesus is so precious."

The one standing with him said, "You've already said Jesus is precious."

To which Newton responded, "I know I have said it, and I will say it again." Then in a strong voice he thundered, "Jesus is so precious."

Application

Our God wants us to finish this year strongly. But to do that we must decide to follow him with all our heart. It's our God who can make our dreams come true. It's our God who can raise our hopes from the ashes.

3. Third, Caleb was a man of vigor.

Listen to what Caleb says in 14:12

Now therefore give me this mountain, whereof the Lord spoke in that day; for you heard in that day how the Anakims were there, and that the cities were great and fenced: if so be the Lord will be with me, then I shall be able to drive them out, as the Lord said.

Question

What is it that Caleb says he will do? That's right. He will realize God's promise and fulfill his destiny. Who is he counting on to help him? That's right. The Lord is the one on whom he is counting.

May I suggest three reasons for Caleb's confident attitude?

Caleb had learned patience by decades of wilderness wandering. Caleb had learned endurance by staying when things were hard. Caleb had learned to trust God while putting up with the injustice of others.

Application

Now it was payoff time. Caleb knew something all of us need to know or learn. God never disappoints. Just hold on. Just keep working. Just keep going. The walls will fall. Your victories will *come*.

Illustration

One evening an older Christian gentleman was sitting by a window. The older man was watching a lamplighter, torch in hand, igniting the oil lamps on a distant hill.

The lamplighter himself could not be seen. But, his progress could be observed by the succession of lamps that were lighted.

After a few minutes, the older Christian gentleman turned to his friend and said, "That illustrates what I mean by a genuine Christian. You may not know him or see him, but his way has been marked by the lights he leaves by his passing."

Application

Don't you want to be remembered as a person who marked his or her journey through life by the lights left along the way?

Transition

Now let's see the fourth and last truth about Caleb. It's a truth that will help us to finish this year strongly and claim the victories God has for us.

4. Fourth, Caleb was a man of victories.

Question

How did it turn out for this 85 year-old warrior for God? Caleb succeeded in taking Hebron. He continued to conquer the lands all around him. The final picture of Caleb is that of a man fulfilling his vision.

God also intends that we fulfill our hopes and dreams.

Review

Now let's review. What have we learned from Caleb?

1. We've learned that God wants us to not just see things as they are, but to see things as they can be. He wants us to be like Caleb, people of vision.

2. We've learned that God wants us to follow him with a whole heart. He doesn't expect perfection, but he does expect our commitment to him. He wants us to be like Caleb, people of virtue.

3. We've learned that God wants us to persist. He wants us to never give up. He wants us to get up every morning and continue on the path He has marked for us. He wants us to be like Caleb, a people of vigor.

4. Lastly, we've learned that God wants us to fulfill our hopes and dreams. He wants us to be like Caleb, people of victory.

F. Visualization of the Solution

I want to close by telling you about a man who chose to follow the road I have described to you this morning. That road for him became known as, "The Road of the Loving Heart."

His name was Robert Louis Stevenson. He was the famous author of such classics as *Kidnapped, Treasure Island* and *The Strange Case of Dr. Jekyll and Mr. Hyde*.

Stevenson was ill, probably with Tuberculosis. He went to the South Seas to get his health back.

The island was under the control of the Europeans. They imprisoned and mistreated the local Samoans.

Stevenson was a compassionate man. He took food and gifts to those in prison. The people came to love him.

His home was on a bluff above the beach. It was a treacherous climb down to the beach. So out of gratitude to Stevenson, the Samoans built a road from his home down to the beach. They called it, "The Road of the Loving Heart."

Stevenson succumbed to his frail health. At his funeral a young Scotsman stood to say that he owed his life to Stevenson. He told how Stevenson had talked him out of suicide.

The Samoans buried him on one of their mountains. They forbad hunting on the mountain, "So that the birds might sing undisturbed," they said.

Conclusion to the Sermon

Sermon Summary

I think the phrase, he traveled the road of the loving heart, would make a good epitaph for Robert Louis Stevenson, or for any Christian.

I can also think of a good epitaph for Caleb. It would be this: he died climbing. Caleb died climbing because he was a man of vision, virtue, vigor, and victory.

G. Call for Response

When December 31 rolls around, and it will; will you be climbing, or will you be sinking? How will you finish this year? It's not important how you answer me. It's only important how you answer to yourself and to God.

H. Invitation

Invitation to the Church

Do you see this altar? This is a place where we can begin to be like Caleb this morning. I want to encourage you to come to the altar. You may kneel, sit, or stand. I want to encourage you to commit yourselves to finish this year climbing like a Caleb!

Invitation to Membership

I haven't forgotten the invitation with which I opened this sermon. I am going to step down to the front. While people are coming to pray, I want to invite you to come and join this good church. We will assist you in your decision.

Invitation to Faith and Baptism

I have a special word for those who want to begin the Christian journey this morning. This would be a wonderful day to begin to travel the road of the loving heart.

I'm going to pray a prayer. You may listen to it, or you may quietly repeat it with me. It will be a prayer of faith.

"Dear God and Father, Thank you for loving me, and sending Jesus to die on the cross for my sins. I'm sorry for my sinfulness and ask for your forgiveness. Lord Jesus, please come into my heart and my life. I accept you as my Savior and Lord. Amen."

Friend, if you agree with that prayer, then won't you say to the Lord, "Lord, that's my prayer today."

During the hymn of invitation, I invite you to come forward. Give me your hand as a sign that today you gladly confess Jesus Christ as your Savior. We will joyfully receive you and arrange for your baptism.

I. Afterglow

Now to him who is able to do immeasurably more than all we ask or imagine, according to his power that is at work within us, to him be glory in the church and in Christ Jesus.
Ephesians 1:20-21

Follow up

The first Sunday of a new year is an excellent time to launch a year-long program of reading the Bible through. Sign-up cards could be inserted in the bulletin. Sunday school teachers could hand them out in adult and youth classes.

Those signing up could be asked to include email addresses. The Bible reading plans could be emailed to them. Copies might also be available in the Church library and Church office.

The email addresses would make it possible for the pastor to write words of encouragement occasionally to those following the program.

There are several good sources for reading the Bible through in a year. The pastor might select the one he thinks best suited to his congregation.

Chapter 11
Sermon for Easter Sunday

Sermon Abstract

Title: What is on the other side of death?

Scripture: Philippians 3:10-11

Central Truth of Passage

The risen Lord Jesus Christ can give us victory over death and the grave.

Problem/Need to be Resolved

Death is a reality for all. Many of us are not prepared mentally or spiritually to meet this event. For all of those who are unprepared, eternal judgment will mean separation from God and all that is good.

Biblical Solution to the Problem/Need

The Bible teaches that Jesus atoned for our sins on the cross and then rose from the dead. Eternal life is God's gift for those who believe and accept Jesus Christ as Lord and Savior.

Sermon Purpose

To persuade listeners to prepare for death and judgment through faith in the risen Lord Jesus Christ

Introduction to the Sermon

A. Goodwill

Good morning. I am delighted to see you on this Easter Sunday morning. I believe I have a message that will be of interest to every person in the audience.

This morning we will answer the question, "What is on the other side of death?"

You can appreciate why this message will be of interest to you and the people sitting next to you. Death is an experience we are all going to face.

B. Pre-Invitation

At the conclusion of the message this morning there will be a hymn of invitation. I will be at the front of the sanctuary to welcome and assist those of you who desire to unite with this good church by transfer of membership.

Some may want to use this occasion to make a public confession of faith in our Lord Jesus Christ. We will receive you joyfully upon your decision and arrange for your baptism.

Now I know that there are many reasons why we are here today. Would you grant me one request? God has promised to be among us. Would each of you be open to hear His voice? Thank you.

C. Attention

Humor

Do you ever read the obituaries in the newspaper? I do occasionally. I usually check on Muskogee where I was born and raised. Then I check on Collinsville where I was pastor for 23 years.

I heard of one fellow who read the obituaries every morning while he was having his morning coffee. One morning he was shocked to see his name listed in the obituary column. He dialed up his best friend immediately.

"Have you read the morning paper?" he asked.

"Yes," said his friend.

"Did you see my name in the obituaries," the man inquired.

"Yes," his friend replied. Then there was a long pause. Finally, the silence was broken when the friend asked, "Where are you calling from?"

Body of the Sermon

D. Problem/Need to be Resolved

Death is a reality for all of us. Are you prepared mentally and spiritually to meet this event. The Bible tells us what it means to be unprepared. It means an eternal judgment of separation from God and all that is good.

Question

Now let me ask you a far more important question than whether you read the obituaries. If you could call from the other side, i.e., from the other side of death, do you know from where you would be calling? Would it be from a place called heaven, or from a place called hell?

Let's think about what we know. We know we are going to die. One fellow said, "I don't mind dying, I just don't want to be there when it happens." But we are going to be there. That we know.

What happens after death? We're all familiar with the physical side of death. The body ceases to function and grows cold. Eventually it will turn to dust.

The question is, is that it? Is that all? The Bible says it is not. Turn to Philippians 3:10-11:

10 That I may know him, and the power of his resurrection, and the fellowship of his sufferings, being made conformable to his death;

11 If by any means I might attain to the resurrection of the dead.

Explain the Scriptures

Paul writes to the Philippians about his hope after death. And what is that hope? It's absolutely astonishing. Paul hoped to experience the resurrection from the dead. What gave him this hope? It was Christ Jesus.

Just as Christ was raised from the dead, Paul believed that same power would raise him from the dead.

Question

Does the Bible anywhere else talk about what happens when we die? Yes, in many places. Let me cite two.

Look at verses 20-21:

20 For our conversation is in heaven; from where also we look for the Savior, the Lord Jesus Christ:

21 Who shall change our vile body that it may be fashioned like to his glorious body, according to the working whereby he is able even to subdue all things to Himself.

These verses say that heaven is the home of the Christian. On the great day of the Lord our dead and decayed bodies will be transformed into bodies that conform to the gloriously resurrected body of the Lord Jesus.

Then there is this in Hebrews 9:27-28:

27 And as it is appointed to men once to die, but after this the judgment:

28 So Christ was once offered to bear the sins of many; and to them that look for him shall he appear the second time without sin unto salvation.

The Bible says that after death we face judgment. Then in the next verse the Bible tells us how to get ready for that inevitable event.

The Bible points to Christ who died for our sins. He will return one day to raise our dead bodies so that we can be with him, and can be like him.

Problem, Continued

Now I want to ask you what you believe will happen after death? Most people who reject the claims of Christianity think that death is final; that there is nothing on the other side. Death is the end of life, period.

Question

What proof is there for believing death is final? Did someone come back from the other side of death to tell us that? No, obviously not. That would refute the argument wouldn't it? We have no evidence that death is final. But we do have many kinds of evidence that there is life after death.

Transition

What are some of the evidences for life after death? Do they support Paul's belief that he will overcome death and live in heaven with Christ? Let me quickly suggest a few.

1. Archeologists have discovered that ancient civilizations were deeply religious and believed in life after death.

They also have evidence that human beings, whether living in advanced cultures or primitive societies, also hold a common belief in the hereafter.

An example is Native Americans. They inhabited North America before the first Europeans arrived. Though they were composed of many different tribes they had this belief in common. They believed in life after death. It was called the happy hunting ground.

But some skeptics would say that those were ancient peoples who weren't scientific. I ask you to think for a moment about this present American generation. It must be considered to be the most scientifically saturated generation that has ever lived.

Would it surprise you to know that 4 out of 5 Americans believe in life after death?

Application

The point I am making is this. Those who believe that the grave is final are among a small minority of all human beings who have ever lived; and that includes those who are alive today.

If you are one of those people who think death is final; should you be comfortable with that?

Summary

We're talking about evidence that there is life after death: and that Jesus Christ is God's way for us to have everlasting life.

2. There's also the example of the original twelve disciples. Church tradition tells us that 10 of the original disciples of

Jesus, men who had seen him alive after his death on the cross, died as martyrs preaching that Jesus had risen from the dead.

The Apostle Paul also endured tremendous physical abuse because he believed and taught that Jesus was raised from the dead.

I ask you, "Would these men have risked physical harm and death for a lie? Would you?"

Application

The only reasonable conclusion is that they believed what their eyes saw, and what their ears heard. They saw and heard the risen Lord. They chose to die rather than deny what they absolutely knew to be true.

3. Then there is the absolute reasonableness of the resurrection. Jesus had to rise from the dead.

You may ask, "Why?"

Think about it. The Bible teaches that Jesus died on the cross as the perfect man sacrificing himself to atone for the sins of the world. That world included you and me. Then the Bible says he was buried.

How do we know he was the perfect man? How do we know he was dying as the perfect sacrifice for our sins? How do we know that God accepted his sacrifice for our sins?

There was only one way for humanity to know that Jesus died as the perfect sacrifice for its sins. That way was an empty tomb in Jerusalem. It shouted to the world that God had accepted Jesus' sacrifice for the sins of the whole world. Without the empty tomb Jesus is just an interesting figure of history.

Transition

Then there is the argument that the Bible is just a bunch of fables.

4. Would it interest you to know that the facts of the Bible have been scrutinized by scholars for nearly 200 years? What is their conclusion? It is that the facts in the Bible that can be verified have been verified. The Bible is reliably true.

It makes me wonder if those who are skeptical about the claims of the Bible have ever really read the book.

For instance:

Illustration

Writer Lew Wallace was a skeptic who set out to disprove the Bible. Not long after he began to read it to refute it, he ended up believing it. He accepted Jesus Christ as his Lord Savior.

He wrote a book of historical fiction entitled, Ben Hur, which celebrated faith in Christ. Hollywood made a movie by the same title. It won a large number of academy awards. You can still catch it on television, especially around Easter.

Illustration

Another famous skeptic was C.S. Lewis, a professor at Cambridge University, England. Lewis was friends with J.R.R. Tolkien, a Christian writer.

Following an evening of studying and discussing the Bible, C.S. Lewis accepted Jesus Christ as his Savior and Lord.

He is an author of many wonderful books about Christianity. He became one of the most famous 20th century voices advocating and defending the Bible.

Transition

Many skeptics have had their minds changed about the truth of the Bible. The important question this morning is this: are you convinced that there is life after death as the Bible clearly teaches? If so, then what would God have us do this morning?

E. Biblical Solution to the Problem/Need

The Bible teaches that Jesus atoned for our sins on the cross and then rose from the dead. Eternal life is obtained by believing and accepting Jesus Christ as Lord and Savior.

Look again at the verses we are considering this morning:

10 That I may know him, and the power of his resurrection, and the fellowship of his sufferings, being made conformable to his death;

11 If by any means I might attain to the resurrection of the dead.

First, the Bible says we can know the resurrected Lord and the power of His resurrection.

Secondly, the Bible teaches that we can obtain life after death by embracing, or becoming one, with Jesus Christ in his sufferings. That speaks of believing that Jesus came on a mission to suffer and die for sins, yours and mine.

Listen to Romans 10:9-10:

9 That if you shall confess with your mouth the Lord Jesus, and shall believe in your heart that God has raised him from the dead, you shall be saved.

10 For with the heart man believes to righteousness; and with the mouth confession is made to salvation.

Review

What has been established thus far? It's clearly more reasonable to believe in Jesus and life after death, than it is to not believe it.

We have established that the way to be ready for the experience of death is to believe in Jesus Christ as Lord and Savior, and to confess him publicly.

Transition

As we come to the end of this message let me ask you the most vital question of the morning. What will be in your mind at the very moment that your heart stops? Will you be ready?

F. Visualization of the Solution

Illustration

May I tell you of a man who wasn't ready for death? But this man got ready for death and left us a wonderful story of inspiration.

His name was John Bunyan and he lived in 17th century England. John Bunyan was an unbeliever.

He married a godly woman named Margaret. Because of Margaret, he began to read the Bible. Bunyan became a Christian and a Puritan preacher.

He was told to stop preaching and he refused. He was then imprisoned for 12 years.

It was during this imprisonment that he began his most famous writing, an allegory entitled, *Pilgrim's Progress*. The book was for many years the second bestselling book in the English speaking world, being outsold only by the Bible.

The book tells about the journey of two pilgrims, Christian and Hopeful, to the Celestial City which is allegorical of heaven.

At one point, Christian and Hopeful see the Celestial City and know they are near. But they are dismayed when they realize that they must cross a very deep and swollen Jordan River to reach the Celestial City.

The River Jordan is allegorical of death. Just as each of us must pass through death, so Christian and Hopeful must pass through the Jordan.

Quoting from the book:

Now, I further saw that betwixt them and the gate was a river: but there was no bridge to go over; and the river was very deep.

Then they addressed themselves to the water, and entering, Christian began to sink, and crying out to his good friend Hopeful, he said,

"I sink in the deep waters; the billows go over my head; all the waves go over me."

Then said the other,

"Be of good cheer, my brother; I feel the bottom, and it is good."

Sermon Conclusion

Sermon Summary

Jesus Christ is the rock upon which we can and must stand through the experience of death. All other ground is sinking sand. He alone can prepare us for what awaits us on the other side of death.

G. Call for Response

Please bow your heads. If you know you have trusted Jesus and are sure you are going to heaven, please raise your hand. Thank you.

Now if you couldn't raise your hand I have good news for you. The good news is that Jesus Christ has done all that is necessary to give us life after death, and take us to heaven. We don't have to earn or deserve heaven. We couldn't anyway. Heaven is a gift that God gives to you when you trust Jesus as your Savior and Lord.

H. Invitation

Invitation to Faith and Baptism

I'm going to pray a prayer. It's a prayer of faith. Listen to the prayer. If you agree with the prayer, then tell the Lord, "That's my prayer to you."

"Our God and Father, I am a sinner in need of forgiveness. I'm a soul in need of salvation. I repent of my sins and I turn to Jesus Christ to save me and take me to heaven someday. Lord Jesus, come into my life and be my Savior. I'll live for you and serve you the best I can. Amen."

In just a moment we are going to stand. I will step down to the front to receive you and assist you. Please come to me. That is your way of saying,

"I will trust Jesus as my Savior from this moment until I die."

We will joyfully receive you and arrange for your baptism and membership in this Church family.

Invitation to Membership

May I also invite other guests to choose this Easter Sunday to move your membership and life into this good church?

I. Afterglow

And now may the Lord of peace himself, give you peace at all times, in all ways. The Lord be with you until we meet again. Amen.

Chapter 12
Sermon for Pentecost Sunday

Sermon Abstract

Title: What do we do if we're in trouble?

Scripture: Philippians 1:19

Central Truth of the Passage

The Apostle Paul, because of his own life experiences, was able to give the answer to handling really big trouble. The first part is the prayer of others. The second part is the power of the Spirit of Jesus Christ.

Problem/Need to be Resolved

Trouble is a reality of life. There are three classes of people in the world. There are those who are having trouble. Then there are those who have had trouble. Finally, there are those who will have trouble.

Biblical Solution to the Problem/Need

The answer to handling really big trouble has two parts. The first is prayer, the prayer of others. The second is power, the power of the Spirit of Jesus Christ.

Sermon Purpose

To encourage listeners to trust themselves and their problems to the prayers of other Christians; to encourage listeners to yield themselves, and their problems, to the power and presence of Christ's Spirit within each of them

Introduction to the Sermon

A. Goodwill

B. Pre-Invitation

There will be an invitation at the conclusion of the message this morning. I will be at the front of the sanctuary to welcome and assist those of you who desire to unite with this church by transfer of membership.

Some may want to use this occasion to make a public confession of faith in our Lord Jesus Christ. We will receive you and arrange for your baptism.

Now I know that there are many reasons why we are here today. Would you grant me one request? God has promised to be among us. Would each of you be open to hear His voice? Thank you.

C. Attention

This morning I want to talk to you about trouble. Fortunately, this kind of trouble is the kind of trouble you can do something about. I know this because we are going to talk about personal trouble.

I don't want to talk to you about little trouble that all of us can manage. I want to talk to you about the big troubles that overwhelm us.

Let me give you an example of a little trouble that we can all manage.

Humor

There was an article in the "Tulsa World" about a London motorist caught speeding on a camera. The police sent him the picture and a ticket.

So the motorist sent back to the police a picture of a check.

The police, by return mail, sent the motorist a picture of a pair of handcuffs.

A real check was in the return mail. Now that's a little trouble.

Body of the Sermon

Read and Discuss the Scriptures

Now turn to Philippians 1:19; and we'll talk about handling real trouble.

19 For I know that this shall turn to my salvation through your prayer, and the supply of the Spirit of Jesus Christ,

Paul is talking about what had happened to him. He's talking about big trouble. He's been held in prison for several years, awaiting a trial before the Roman Caesar.

What other troubles had plagued Paul? Listen to this from 2 Corinthians 11:24-28:

24 of the Jews five times received I forty stripes save one.

25 Thrice was I beaten with rods, once was I stoned, thrice I suffered shipwreck, a night and a day I have been in the deep;

26 In journeyings often, in perils of waters, in perils of robbers, in perils by mine own countrymen, in perils by the heathen, in perils in the city, in perils in the wilderness, in perils in the sea, in perils among false brethren;

27 In weariness and painfulness, in watchings often, in hunger and thirst, in fastings often, in cold and nakedness.

28 Beside those things that are without, that which cometh upon me daily, the care of all the churches.

Paul's life as a Christian had been a series of difficulties and troubles. But thankfully, he had found the way to handle them.

D. Problem/Need to be Resolved

Can you identify with Paul this morning? Have you known real trouble? I think there are three classes of people in the audience this morning. There are those who are having trouble. Then there are those who have had trouble. Finally, there are those who will have trouble.

Listen to how Paul describes the life of the believer in 2 Corinthians 4.8-10:

8 We are troubled on every side, yet not distressed; we are perplexed, but not in despair;

9 Persecuted, but not forsaken; cast down, but not destroyed;

10 Always bearing about in the body the dying of the Lord Jesus: that the life also of Jesus might be made manifest in our body.

Transition

Does that describe how you have sometimes felt. You may be feeling that way this morning. Would you like to know the secret for handling trouble?

The secret is in this verse, Philippians 1:19,

19 For I know that this shall turn to my salvation through your prayer, and the supply of the Spirit of Jesus Christ,

E. Biblical Solution to the Problem/Need

Do you see it? The answer to handling really big trouble has two parts. The first is prayer. The second is the Spirit of Jesus Christ.

First Part: Prayer

The first part in handling trouble is prayer. Notice the kind of prayer Paul is talking about. Paul is not talking about his prayers. Whose prayers are helping Paul? That's right. The prayers that are helping Paul are the prayers of the Christians at Philippi.

Do you understand prayer? I confess that I don't fully understand prayer. But I do know something about prayer. Prayer is mystical and powerful. Prayer can change people. Prayer can change circumstances and outcomes. Some would even say that prayer can change the mind of God. That's a discussion for another day.

Prayer is one of those graces God has given to us that doesn't have to be understood. I don't think prayer can ever be fully understood. But prayer can and must be employed to handle big trouble.

Second Part: Spirit of Christ

The second part of handling trouble according to Paul is "...the supply of the Spirit of Jesus Christ."

Now when Jesus was on earth he was in an earthly body. He was limited physically to one locality, to one presence. But then he overcame death and the grave, and ascended up to heaven.

On the Day of Pentecost he poured out his Spirit upon all who were believers. That meant that he could be with them regardless of time or place.

When you accepted Jesus as Lord and Savior Jesus promised to be with you and never leave you. And as Paul has observed in the scriptures, the Spirit of Christ will give us help and deliver us.

Question

What kind of helps might the Spirit of Jesus Christ give to each of us this morning?

Illustrations

Do remember that place in the Book of Judges that tells about Samson meeting a dangerous young lion. The Bible says that the Spirit of God was upon him and he tore the lion apart.

What's remarkable about the story is that there was nothing remarkable about Samson. He was just an ordinary man who had been dedicated to the Lord by his parents. It was the Spirit of God that made Samson strong and able to defeat the lion, and also to defeat the enemies of God's people.

Do you remember, also from the Old Testament, what it was that Elisha requested of the Lord? He asked for a double portion of the Spirit that had enabled his mentor Elijah to defeat the idolatrous king Ahab and evil Queen Jezebel.

Application

Isn't that what we need? Don't we need help that's beyond our ordinary strength and ability?

Illustrations

The New Testament book of "Acts" is filled with stories of ordinary people doing extraordinary things.

1. Peter, a fisherman filled with Christ's Spirit, preached with such power on Pentecost that 3,000 souls were saved (Acts 2:40-41).

2. Stephen, being filled with the Holy Spirit, witnessed fearlessly and was martyred for his faith (Acts 7:55-56).

3. Saul had been a persecutor of Christians. He was filled with the Holy Spirit and became Paul, the Apostle to the Gentiles (Acts 9:17).

Application

The Spirit of Jesus Christ can help us with whatever it is that we may be facing at this moment, whether it be physical, emotional or spiritual trouble.

The Spirit of Jesus Christ enables ordinary people to do extraordinary things.

F. Visualization of the Solution

Illustration

Let me give you a modern day example of a man who found help for trouble in his life. His name is Travis Fryman and his story was reported in the "Daily Oklahoman," 03/24/01, Pp. 1-2B.

Travis Fryman was an all-star third baseman and shortstop in the 90s, for the Cleveland Indians and Detroit Tigers. He retired in 2002.

Fryman said, "Most adults don't come to Christ unless they are in some sort of crisis. All of us want a sense of peace, a sense of purpose, and I have that now."

Fryman was the leader of the Cleveland Indians baseball chapel. But his journey to that ministry to his fellow players was most unlikely.

He describes himself as the infant terrible of baseball. He said it was true of him from the time he was a small boy. He still doesn't know where all the anger came from...but he had it and it exploded often.

If he struck out the other players moved to the far end of the bench away from him. He would curse and throw things. He carried the game home and took it out on his young wife, Kathleen. She couldn't handle his moods.

Then, in the summer of 1992 Cathy Tanana, the wife of Cleveland Indians pitcher Frank Tanana, led Kathleen to the Lord, in the parking lot of the baseball stadium.

Travis could see the changes in his young wife. She was calmer, more able to cope. He began to attend church with her. Church had just been a religious exercise before. Now it took on meaning.

He said, "I finally realized that I had to stop playing baseball for myself, and realized that my talent was a gift from God. I was playing for him."

He made a commitment to Jesus Christ. He began to read the Bible and he cleaned up his mouth. He brought his temper under control with the help of God.

The other players waited for the explosion to come, for the old Travis to reappear. He never did. Even when he went into a prolonged slump at bat he didn't give in to anger.

He said, "I see that as a time of testing. It made me stronger." So the infant terrible of Major League Baseball led Bible study every week.

His goal is "not to preach, but to make an invisible God visible to the people who come into contact with me."

Conclusion to the Sermon

Sermon Summary

The Apostle Paul, one of the greatest Christians who ever lived, has given us a golden answer to handling trouble. **First**, he says we need the prayers of other Christians. **Second**, he says we need the help of the Spirit of Jesus Christ.

The Apostle Paul experienced the mighty help of Christ's Spirit again and again. Travis Fryman experienced God's help and became a changed man.

G. Call for Response

Question

Now, how can you leave the service this morning with the help you need for your troubles?

First, by being under the influence and control of the Spirit of Jesus Christ who will help you with your troubles

Second, by having this church family to pray for you

H. Invitation

In just a moment I'm going to invite those who want and need Christ's help, to stand at your seat. When all have responded who will, I'm going to pray for you.

First, I'm going to pray that the Spirit of Jesus Christ will fill you and give you every heavenly help that is needed at this time.

Secondly, I'm going to ask this church family to make a commitment to pray for you. I know they will do it. And I know God will hear their prayers for you.

Question

Now it's up to us isn't it? We can carry our burden alone, sadly and in suffering silence. Or we can seek the help of the Spirit of Christ. And we can ask for and receive the prayers of this church family?

Prayer Time

Please, every head bowed. Now my dear friend, please stand if you want the help of our Lord Jesus Christ this morning.

Give time for people to stand.

We're going to ask the Spirit of Christ to come into each of us and help us. Before we ask that, we need to cleanse our hearts by confessing our sins privately.

Prayer: Lead a prayer of forgiveness and cleansing.

Now I'm going to ask the Spirit of Christ to fill you. Open your hearts now and make room for him as I pray.

Prayer: Pray for the filling of the Spirit of Jesus Christ for those who are standing.

Now I want to ask this church family to pray for you. Please, Church family, look about you at these who are standing. Please rise and go to them. Place your hand on their shoulder and pray for them.

Prayer: Lead a prayer of intercession for those who are standing.

Invitation to Faith and Baptism

Please stand for the time of invitation. I want to extend an invitation to those of you who want Jesus Christ in your life.

I want to invite you to come forward. We will assist you. Coming forward is your way of saying, "I need the forgiveness and help that Christ alone can give. I will trust Him as my Savior."

Invitation to Church Membership

I also want to invite those who want to join this good church. Please come forward. We will joyfully receive you and assist you.

I. Afterglow

Irish Blessing: May the road rise to meet you and the wind be always at your back. May the sun shine warm upon your face. And rains fall soft upon your fields. And until we meet again, the Lord God hold you in the hollow of his hand. Amen.

Chapter 13
Sermon for Mother's Day

Sermon Abstract

Title: What if you're filled with bitterness and anguish?

Scripture Passage: I Samuel 1:10-20

Central Truth of the Passage

Hannah had many reasons to be content. But she was filled with bitterness and anguish. Hannah learned that genuine happiness comes when we find and do God's will

Problem/Need to be Resolved

It's quite possible for Christians, though they have many reasons to be content, to find themselves filled with bitterness and anguish.

What might be the cause of such unhappiness? Is there a remedy?

Biblical Solution to the Problem

The way out of bitterness and anguish is to find and do God's will. That is the path to peace and genuine happiness.

Sermon Purpose

To encourage listeners to find the peace and joy that comes to our troubled hearts when we say to our God, "Thy will be done!"

Introduction to the Sermon

A. Goodwill

Americans have been honoring Mother's Day since May 9, 1914. That's when President Woodrow Wilson issued a proclamation that declared the second Sunday in May to be Mother's Day throughout America.

Quote

I love this description of a mother penned by an unknown author:

A mother can be almost any size or any age, but she won't admit to anything over thirty. A mother has soft hands and smells good. A mother likes new dresses, music, a clean house, her children's kisses, an automatic washer, and flowers.

A mother doesn't like having her children sick, muddy feet, temper tantrums, loud noise or bad report cards. A mother can read a thermometer (much to the amazement of Daddy) and, like magic, can kiss a hurt away.

A mother can bake good cakes and pies, but likes to see her children eat vegetables. A mother can stuff a fat baby into a snowsuit in seconds, and can kiss sad little faces and make them smile.

A mother is underpaid, has long hours, and gets very little rest. She worries too much about her children; but she says she doesn't mind at all. And no matter how old her children are, she still likes to think of them as her little babies.

She is the guardian angel of the family, the queen, the tender hand of love. A mother is the best friend anyone ever has. A mother is love."

B. Pre-Invitation

There will be an invitation at the conclusion of the message this morning. I will be at the front of the sanctuary to welcome and assist those of you who desire to unite with this church by transfer of membership.

This would be a wonderful occasion to make a public confession of faith in our Lord Jesus Christ. We will receive you joyfully upon your decision and arrange for your baptism.

Now I know that there are many reasons why we are here today. God has promised to be among us. Would each of you be open to hear His voice? Thank you.

C. Attention

Motherhood is the most challenging job in the world. Mothers give birth to their babies and love them even though they're brought forth through great pain. They nurture and care for their children at great personal sacrifice.

Humor

One mother of three notoriously unruly youngsters was asked, "If you could do it all over again, would you still have children?"

"Yes," she replied, "But not the same ones."

A pastor was visiting a mother of three when the youngest, a four-year-old, walked in covered with mud from head to toe.

The understanding pastor said, "Would you like to take time to clean him up?"

The mother replied solemnly, "Pastor, it would be quicker to just make another one."

113

Transition

Now turn in your Bibles to I Samuel 1:10-20. We're going to talk about a woman named Hannah. She wanted to be a mother more than anything else in the world. Her story will help us to find the answer to a perplexing question.

Body of the Sermon

D. Problem/Need to be Resolved

It's possible for Christians who have many reasons to be content, to find themselves filled with bitterness and anguish.

Question: What do you do if you're filled with bitterness and anguish? That was the situation with Hannah who is the subject of our Bible study this morning.

Read I Samuel 1:10-20

10 And she was in bitterness of soul, and prayed to the Lord, and wept in anguish.

11 And she vowed a vow, and said, "O Lord of hosts, if You will indeed look on the affliction of your handmaid, and remember me, and not forget your handmaid, but wilt give to your handmaid a man child, then I will give him to the Lord all the days of his life, and there shall no razor come upon his head."

12 And it came to pass, as she continued praying before the Lord, that Eli marked her mouth.

13 Now Hannah spoke in her heart; only her lips moved, but her voice was not heard: therefore Eli thought she was drunk with wine.

14 And Eli said to her, "How long will you be drunk? Put away your wine from you."

15 And Hannah answered and said, "No, my lord, I am a woman of a sorrowful spirit: I have drunk neither wine nor strong drink, but have poured out my soul before the Lord. 16 Count not your handmaid for a daughter of Belial: for out of the abundance of my complaint and grief have I spoken."

17 Then Eli answered and said, "Go in peace and the God of Israel give to you the petition that you have asked of him."

And she said, "Let your handmaid find grace in your sight." So the woman went her way, and did eat, and her countenance was no longer sad.

19 And they rose up in the morning early, and worshipped before the Lord, and returned, and came to their house to Ramah: and Elkanah knew Hannah his wife; and the Lord remembered her.

20 Wherefore it came to pass, when the time was come about after Hannah had conceived, that she bare a son, and called his name Samuel, saying, "Because I have asked him of the Lord."

Background: I Samuel 1:10-20

It's the time after the settlement of Canaan by the Israelite tribes. The period is known as the time of the Judges. That period was drawing to a close. Soon the time of the Kings would begin. Saul would be anointed as the first king of Israel. He would be followed by the famous King David.

The transitional figure between the two periods would be a man named Samuel. He would be the final judge of Israel. He would anoint both Saul and David as kings over Israel.

The place of worship was the tent tabernacle at Shiloh. Jerusalem hadn't yet fallen into the hands of God's people.

Explain the Scripture Passage

Today's Bible study is about Hannah, the mother of Samuel. Where is Hannah in our story? She's at the Lord's tabernacle (tent) in Shiloh.

What is Hannah doing? She's worshiping the Lord with her family. They have eaten a meal just outside the tabernacle enclosure.

Who else is there? Eli the high priest is there observing the worshippers. He's acting in his role as overseer of the tent of worship. But as high priest his primary role is one of intercession for the people to God.

What do we know about Hannah? She was a godly woman given to prayer and worship of God. She was married to a man of the Tribe of Levi. Elkanah, her husband, also belonged to one of the best families in the tribe. It was a prosperous family.

Elkanah was a good and kind man. Hannah was much loved by her husband. He would have done anything for her.

Yet in our story Hannah isn't happy. Look at verse 10:

¹⁰And she was in bitterness of soul, and prayed to the LORD and wept in anguish.

What's the cause of Hannah's condition? She's in bitterness and anguish because she's childless. The depth of her agony is being expressed through her tears.

Review

Let's review the question for which we are seeking an answer.

Question: We know that God wants peace and joy for those who follow him. Hannah had neither. What do you do if you're filled with bitterness and anguish?

What did Hannah do?

She went to the tent tabernacle at Shiloh and she prayed. She prayed until she was oblivious to anything but God. Eli saw her in this state and thought she had succumbed to wine.

What is it that brought this good, godly woman to this state? I believe it's this. God had placed the desire to be a mother in the heart of Hannah. But Hannah was barren. The tension between Hannah's natural desire to be a mother and the reality of her barrenness had created this anguish of soul.

Transition

Is there an answer to our question, "What do you do if you're filled with bitterness and anguish?"

E. Biblical Solution to the Problem/Need

Answer: Discover what God wants. Accept his will. Then peace and joy can reign in your heart.

Notice Hannah's prayer in verse 11.

[11] Then she made a vow and said, "O LORD of hosts, if you will indeed look on the affliction of your maidservant and remember me, and not forget your maidservant, but will give your maidservant a male child, then I will give him to the LORD all the days of his life, and no razor shall come upon his head."

How did she address the Lord? She called him The Lord of hosts. This meant that she understood that the Lord was mighty and commanded a vast heavenly army to do his will.

What else did she do? For the privilege of motherhood she agreed to give up the son she had requested from God. She would give him back to God to serve in the holy place at Shiloh.

117

Application

Hannah was now in the center of God's will. She would become the mother of Samuel, the man God would use during a crucial period of transition in the history of Israel.

Now let's read the story again and see the amazing transformation in Hannah.

¹²And it happened, as she continued praying before the LORD, that Eli watched her mouth.

¹³Now Hannah spoke in her heart; only her lips moved, but her voice was not heard. Therefore Eli thought she was drunk.

¹⁴So Eli said to her, "How long will you be drunk? Put your wine away from you!"

¹⁵But Hannah answered and said, "No, my lord, I am a woman of sorrowful spirit. I have drunk neither wine nor intoxicating drink, but have poured out my soul before the LORD.

¹⁶Do not consider your maidservant a wicked woman, for out of the abundance of my complaint and grief I have spoken until now."

¹⁷Then Eli answered and said, "Go in peace, and the God of Israel grant your petition which you have asked of Him."

¹⁸Then Hannah said "Let your maidservant find favor in your sight." So the woman went her way and ate, and her face was no longer sad.

Application

Hannah was no longer sad! Hannah discovered a liberating truth. It's not what we want that gives us peace and joy. It's discovering what God wants and coming into agreement with it. That's what sets us free from bitterness and anguish.

May I sum up Hannah's frame of mind after this prayer: It's this, "Lord, thy will be done."

Transition: What's the rest of the story?

> *[19] Then they rose early in the morning and worshiped before the LORD, and returned and came to their house at Ramah. And Elkanah knew Hannah his wife, and the LORD remembered her.*

> *[20] So it came to pass in the process of time that Hannah conceived and bore a son, and called his name Samuel, saying, "Because I have asked for him from the LORD."*

Conclusion to the Story

When Samuel was old enough Hannah brought him to Shiloh. Samuel remained at Shiloh to serve the Lord. He grew into the prophet, priest, and judge who would take Israel from a community of tribes to a nation under King David.

What became of Hannah? She lent one little son, Samuel, to God because it was God's will. Each year she returned to Shiloh and the tent of God to see her son. Hannah would bring the growing boy a new suit of clothes.

Think of how proud she and Elkanah were of this son. They could see him assuming more and more of the responsibilities of a priest before God.

And God blessed her with an additional three sons and two daughters!

Transition

Now we know the story of Hannah and her journey out of bitterness and anguish into peace and joy. What is your story? Are you filled with bitterness and anguish? What can you do about it?

What would happen if you wrote the same conclusion to your story that Hannah wrote for her story?

What if you took your troubles to the Lord and said, "Father, what I've wanted hasn't made me happy. I haven't asked what you want. Now I'm asking. Lord, I truly want your will to be done in my life."

F. Visualization of the Solution

Illustration

I was a young pastor in Illinois when I visited a home with father, mother, and five children. The youngest, about 5 years-of-age, was crippled from the waist down.

I invited them to church.

The mother said, "Pastor, it's all I can do to take care of these children. I simply can't get them ready and bring them to church. You can see that, can't you?"

I agreed that she had her hands full. I prepared to leave and we had a moment for prayer.

I prayed, "Lord, you have greatly blessed this dear mother with beautiful children. Sometimes they are more than she can handle. I ask you to give her grace and strength for her mother's heart. Amen."

When I looked up she had a most serious look on her face.

She said, "Pastor, God hasn't given me more than I can do. My children are not too much for me. If I can get them ready for school, then I can get them ready for church. We'll be there Sunday."

Over time, one by one, those beautiful children came to a saving faith in Jesus Christ. I still remember the night of a revival service when the youngest came to Christ.

That dear mother came up to me and said, "Pastor, that's the last one. All my children are saved."

"Yes," I said. "It's because of you dear mother, that all of your children have become Christians."

Application

Dear friend, Hannah's story can be your story. You can find peace where there is now unhappiness. It happens when, like Hannah, we stop wanting what we want and start wanting what God wants. It begins to happen when we pray, "Lord, what do you want? What is your will for my life?"

Quote: Many years ago a mother prayed:

"Help me, Lord, to remember that religion is not to be confined to the church, nor exercised only in prayer and meditation, but that everywhere I am, I am in Thy Presence."

That mother was Susannah Wesley, mother of John and Charles Wesley. She is called the mother of Methodism.

Conclusion to the Sermon

Sermon Summary

Hannah had many reasons to be content, but was filled with bitterness and anguish. This morning we have all learned what she learned.

121

Genuine happiness comes when we are in agreement with God's will for our lives.

G. Call for Response

Listen to a prayer that exemplifies the spirit of Hannah. It's a prayer for those who want peace and joy instead of bitterness and anguish.

"Father, what I've wanted hasn't made me happy. I haven't asked what you want. Now I'm asking. Lord, I truly want your will to be done in my life. Amen."

H. Invitation

Invitation to Church Family

I want all to bow in prayer. If the prayer that I just read expresses what's in your heart, I want you to rise and just stand where you are. If you believe that genuine happiness comes when we're in agreement with God's will, and that's what you want, please stand.

God bless you. We are going to pray that the joy and peace that Hannah experienced will also come to you. Let us pray.

"Father, I ask you to reveal your will to each one who is standing. They desire the peace, joy, and purpose that is for those who surrender to your good and perfect will. Amen."

Instruction: Now please, everyone stand for the invitation hymn. The altar is open to any who may want to come kneel, sit or stand in further prayer.

Invitation to Membership

The invitation is extended to Christians who may desire membership in this good church; please come now and let me welcome and assist you.

Invitation to Faith and Baptism

Mother's Day is a wonderful occasion to personally confess Jesus Christ as Lord and Savior. God's word tells us that it is not God's will that any should be lost, but that all should be saved.

Peace, joy and purpose can't be fully known until Jesus is Savior and Lord.

We will receive you joyfully upon your decision and arrange for your baptism. Come now.

I. Afterglow

May the Lord bless you and keep you; the Lord make his face shine upon you and be gracious to you; the Lord turn his face toward you and give you peace.
Numbers 6:24-26

Chapter 14
Sermon for Father's Day

Sermon Abstract

Title: What is the right way?

Scripture: Ecclesiastes 12:13

> *13 Let us hear the conclusion of the whole matter: Fear God, and keep his commandments: for this is the whole duty of man.*

Central Truths of the Passage

King Solomon was very likely near the end of his life. He wanted his son and the people to avoid his mistakes. He wrote down the wisdom that he had learned from God. Solomon also recorded what he had learned from the school of hard knocks.

King Solomon said, *"Fear God and keep his commandments."* The right way to live begins with a respectful awe of God. The right path of life is guarded and guided by God's commandments.

Problem/Need to be Resolved

There are many choices in life. Many lead to unhappiness and disaster. How can we find the right way to live?

Biblical Solution to the Problem/Need

King Solomon said, *"Fear God and keep his commandments."* His scriptural prescription for life was:

1. Lead a life of faith in God.

2. Lead a life of obedience to God.

Sermon Purpose

To encourage listeners to commit to faith in God and a life of obedience to God

Introduction to the Sermon

A. Goodwill

Good morning on this Father's Day. Would you like to know how to be a father, or a man or a woman, who pleases God?

I believe I have a message from God's word that is full of wisdom. It can help us to live lives pleasing to God, and lives that are a blessing to those who love us.

Transition: Please turn in your Bibles to Ecclesiastes 12:13.

B. Pre-Invitation

There will be an invitation at the conclusion of the message this morning. I will be at the front of the sanctuary to welcome and assist those of you who desire to unite with this church by transfer of membership.

Some may want to use this occasion to make a public confession of faith in our Lord Jesus Christ. We will receive you and arrange for your baptism.

Now I know that there are many reasons why we are here today. God has promised to be among us. Would each of you be open to hear His voice? Thank you.

C. Attention

13 Let us hear the conclusion of the whole matter: Fear God, and keep his commandments: for this is the whole duty of man.

Explain the Verse

When I read the book of Ecclesiastes I'm filled with great sadness. King Solomon very likely wrote this book near the end of his life. He wrote it for his people, but especially for his son.

When Solomon reviewed the way he had lived he concluded that his life had missed the mark. Isn't that sad?

He openly acknowledged his mistakes and issued many warnings in the 12 chapters of the book.

He said:

1. Don't make wealth a god. Don't spend your life accumulating wealth for its own sake. Everyone, rich or poor, will die and leave everything.

Enjoy what you have, but don't make the mistake of living for what you have. There is no purpose or happiness in that. 5:10, 13

2. Don't live for pleasure. Don't spend your life pursuing sensual pleasures. They will leave you exhausted and empty. 2:10-11

3. Don't just live for the physical side of your being. Enjoy health, beauty, and youth, but realize that they will fade. They're not the purpose for life, nor will they give happiness. 11:9-10; 12:1

4. Don't live for causes. Crusading against injustice is a good thing; but it can't be the meaning of life. Life isn't fair. Injustice will always exist. 3:16; 5:8

5. Don't expect others to make you happy. Enjoy the companionship of others but don't depend upon them for your

happiness. People may prove to be unreliable.
7:28

6. Don't turn off to life. Solomon uses the word, "vanity," 37 times to describe life. You can become cynical about life. But there is no happiness in that.
2:18-20; 12:6

Application

Solomon had done all of these things and he hadn't found happiness in any of them. Now a son would follow him to the throne. He doesn't want his son, or the people, to follow his example.

Illustration

There is a lighthouse on the coast of Massachusetts. It flashes its warning to ships at sea. There's a pattern to the signals. The lights spell out in Morse code, "I love you."

The Coast Guard decided to install new equipment that flashed no message. There was such a protest that the Coast Guard backed off. The old equipment is still in use, still signaling its message, "I love you."

Application

Solomon warned his son away from the things that are meaninglessness and empty of happiness. He didn't want anyone to follow his failed example.

Body of the Sermon

D. Problem/Need to be Resolved

There are many choices in life. Many lead to unhappiness and disaster. We need to ask ourselves, "How can I find the right way to live?"

Transition: That brings us to our key verse this morning. Solomon concluded his book by the advice he hoped everyone would follow.

E. Biblical Solution to the Problem/Need

King Solomon summed up everything by saying, "Fear God and keep his commandments."

The two goals of life are:

1. To have faith in God

2. To live a life of obedience to God

Transition

What does it mean to have faith in God? It means to commit one's life into the hands of God. It means to allow God to be in control and to follow his leading.

F. Visualization of the Solution

Part One: Faith in God

Illustration

Pistol Pete Maravich was one of the greatest basketball players in the history of the game.

Pete tried everything to find peace and contentment. He tried every kind of religion. He tried every kind of diet and self-denial. Yes, he also tried every kind of dissipation. Then the shadow of Jesus fell across his life and he put his life in Jesus' hands.

From that time on he was a better man, a better husband, and a better father. He took his own father, dying of cancer, into his home and cared for him during the last year of his life. He won his dad to a personal faith in the Lord.

Pete died playing a pickup game of basketball at a church. The autopsy showed something amazing. The left side of his heart was not fully developed. Pete had only half a heart. He had done the most amazing things on the basketball court with just half a heart.

But his biographers must write that God gave him a new heart, a spiritual heart that brought him profound peace, and greatly influenced many others.

One of the last acts he ever did was to send a Bible to CNN's Larry King. Pete had appeared on Larry's television show. The Bible was personally inscribed and gave witness to Pete's faith.

I heard Larry King say about Pete, "He was truly born again!"

Application

Solomon said that the way to a happy and meaningful life was through faith in God. Pete Maravich had that kind of faith.

Transition

Solomon went on to say that a happy and meaningful life was a life lived in obedience to God.

Part Two: Live in obedience to God

Question

Are you happy? Is your life fulfilled? If the answer is, "No," could it be because you are living in some way that is displeasing to God.

Illustration

Roy Angel, a Christian author and Florida pastor, told the story of Dr. Glenn Clark, college educator and author of devotional books.

Dr. Clark's life had become confused. His ambitions were thwarted. Finally, he was near nervous collapse. His doctor sent him out West to recover. He lived and worked on a real ranch. He worked beside genuine cowhands.

He went along with the cowboys as they took some salt up to the cattle on number six mesa. The group paused at number five mesa. The Cowboys told Dr. Clark he could go no farther.

They said, "Our horses are chosen because they are surefooted. They have feet like deer. They can climb anything. They track."

"Your horse's hindquarters don't track. Notice how my horse's rear hooves fall exactly in the track of the front. Your horse's hooves don't do that," they explained.

The Cowboys had not gone far when Dr. Clark dismounted. He got down on his knees. He began to thank God for the simple lesson that would change his life.

You see, Dr. Clark's life didn't track. There were cross-pulls that he had not and would not acknowledge to God.

He prayed, "God help me to track. Help my life to track."

"I was cured," He said "The tug-of-war within him was gone."

Application

This was the problem in the Bible with men like King Saul, Samson, Pharaoh and Judas. Their lives wouldn't track. Thus, instead of becoming heroes like James and John, Peter and Paul, they became characters of infamy.

Transition: Let's review what we have learned this morning.

Conclusion to the Sermon

Sermon Summary

King Solomon wrote Ecclesiastes to warn his son and his people about paths in life that lead to unhappiness.

1. He warned them not to make wealth a god.

2. He warned them of the emptiness of living for pleasure.

3. He reminded them that health, beauty and youth would fade away.

4. He encouraged them to right injustices, but to remember that such injustices would always exist.

5. He told them to enjoy the companionship of others, but to realize that others could not make them happy.

6. Finally, he warned them that becoming cynical and indifferent to the disappointments of life was not a pathway to happiness.

Transition

Then he gave them the path to a happy and meaningful life out of his own personal experience.

First, he told them that a happy and meaningful life required faith in God.

Second, he told them that a happy and meaningful life required a life lived in obedience to God.

Transition

I believe our Father in Heaven would have us to acknowledge Solomon's wisdom on this Father's Day.

G. Call for Response

Some of us are like Pistol Pete Maravich. We will never find happiness and the meaning for our lives until we put our lives into the hands of the Lord Jesus Christ.

Some of us are like Glenn Clark, the doctor. There are cross pulls in our lives. Our lives don't track. These cross pulls are robbing us of happiness and eternal purpose. God is calling on all of us to commit to a life of obedience this morning.

H. Invitation

Invitation to Faith and Baptism

Please bow your heads for a moment. If, like Pistol Pete Maravich, you have committed your life to Jesus Christ and have trusted him for your eternal salvation, then please raise your hand for a moment. Thank you.

I'm stepping down to the front for our time of invitation.

First, I would like to speak a word to those of you who didn't raise your hand. I want to invite you to come forward on this Father's Day and declare your faith in the Lord Jesus Christ. He will forgive you and save you.

He will never leave you or forsake you. I'm offering you my hand. Let our handshake be a sign that you will trust him as your Lord and Savior. This good church will arrange for your baptism and church membership.

Invitation to Christians

Next, I want to speak to Christians here today who will follow the example of Dr. Clark. Please come forward and find a place here at the altar. Tell the Lord that you will, with his help, do the very best you can to be obedient to his word and way.

Invitation to Membership

Lastly, I want to invite those who desire to unite with this church to come forward. We will welcome you with friendship and love.

I. Afterglow

And now may the love of God, and the peace of our Lord Jesus Christ, and the fellowship of the Holy Spirit abide with you now and forever more. Amen.

Chapter 15
Sermon for Fall Roundup

Sermon Abstract

Title: What do you do if you have that lost feeling?

Scripture: Luke 19:1-10

Central Truth of the Passage

Jesus came to seek and to save those who were lost. Zacchaeus was lost. He was a man lacking personal peace, spiritual purpose, and a place in God's family.

Jesus saved Zacchaeus and gave him peace, purpose and place.

Problem/Need to be Resolved

The Bible describes those without Jesus Christ as personally lost. They also lack abiding peace and a sense of spiritual purpose. They have no assurance that there is a place for them in God's family.

Biblical Solution to the Problem/Need

Jesus is the answer for those who are seeking abiding peace, spiritual purpose, and a place in God's heavenly family.

Sermon Purpose

To use the story of Zacchaeus to encourage listeners to look to Christ for personal peace, spiritual purpose, and a place in God's family

Introduction to the Sermon

A. Goodwill

Summer is ending and school is beginning. Today is Fall roundup. It's time to launch out on a program of Sunday School and Church growth. We're off to a good start thanks to all who attended this morning.

There are still a lot of lost doggies out there to be rounded up. It's no fun being lost. That's the subject of the morning message.

Transition: Now, turn in your Bibles to Luke 19:1-10.

B. Pre-Invitation

There will be an invitation at the conclusion of the message this morning. I will be at the front of the sanctuary to welcome and assist those of you who desire to unite with this church by transfer of membership.

Some may want to use this occasion to make a public confession of faith in our Lord Jesus Christ. We will receive you and arrange for your baptism.

Now I know that there are many reasons why we are here today. God has promised to be among us. Would each of you be open to hear His voice? Thank you.

C. Attention

This morning we are going to look at a surprising encounter Jesus had with a man named Zacchaeus. I say surprising because Jesus had to get Zacchaeus down out of a tree.

Humor

I heard of another surprising encounter by a minister who was visiting in the community. He stepped onto the porch of a modest house and knocked on the door. A boy about ten years of age came to the door.

The minister asked, "Is your mother at home?" "She's not here," said the boy. "Where is she," asked the minister? The boy said, "Oh, she's in the asylum."

"Is your father here?" the minister asked. "No," said the boy, "he's not here." "Where is he," asked the pastor? The boy said, "He's in jail."

The minister then asked, "Do you have an older brother or sister?" "I got both," replied the boy.

"May I speak to your sister?" The boy said, "She's not here." Where is your sister?" asked the minister? The boy replied, "She ran off to the circus."

"Can I speak to your brother?" asked the pastor. "He's not here," said the boy. The pastor said, "Where is your brother?" "Oh, he's at Harvard," answered the boy.

"Your brother's at Harvard University," the minister said with incredulity! "Yup," said the boy, "they got him there so they can study him."

Transition

Now let's get back to the unusual encounter recorded in the Bible. Someone tell me what the name of Jesus means? That's right. The name means Savior, or to save.

What does the encounter between Jesus and Zacchaeus reveal about our Lord's earthly mission? It tells us that Jesus came for the specific purpose of seeking and saving what was lost.

[10] For the Son of Man came to seek and to save what was lost."

Question

Have you ever been physically lost? How did you feel? Did you feel anxious? Did you feel frightened? Did you feel stupid? Did you feel all of these things?

Illustration

One of my children gave me a GPS device for Christmas. You're thinking, "That child really loves Bro. Wana." I hope so.

But the reason it was given to me is that I get lost. I get lost a lot. I even lose my car in parking lots. The GPS doesn't help me much with that.

Now this isn't an age thing. I kept my poor parents in poverty by the number of coats, hats, and gloves I continually misplaced when I was a youngster.

Application

I'm very familiar with the feeling of being lost and it isn't pleasant. You're anxious and have no peace. You're wandering about without a certain direction. You're not where you're supposed to be.

Body of the Sermon

D. Problem/Need to be Resolved

Zacchaeus was a man who had lost personal peace. He had lost his divine purpose for life. Zacchaeus was an outcast from the Jewish religion. He was adrift in life, having lost his way, his peace, and his place.

Wouldn't it be wonderful if all of us could have personal peace this morning? Wouldn't it be wonderful to know that we're living out our purpose in this world? Wouldn't it be wonderful to know that we're exactly where God wants us to be?

E. Biblical Solution to the Problem/Need

In one brief encounter with Jesus life totally changed for Zacchaeus. Zacchaeus became a man at peace; a man with a sense of purpose, and a man in the place where God wanted him to be.

A quick examination of the story will help us understand how this remarkable transformation occurred.

Read the Scripture Passage: Luke 19:1-10

1 And Jesus entered and passed through Jericho. 2 And, behold, there was a man named Zacchaeus, which was the chief among the publicans, and he was rich.

3 And he sought to see Jesus who he was; and could not for the press, because he was little of stature. 4 And he ran before, and climbed up into a sycamore tree to see him: for he was to pass that way.

5 And when Jesus came to the place, he looked up, and saw him, and said to him, "Zacchaeus, make haste, and come down; for today I must abide at your house." 6 And he made haste, and came down, and received him joyfully.

7 And when they saw it, they all murmured, saying that he was gone to be guest with a man that is a sinner.

8 And Zacchaeus stood, and said to the Lord: "Behold, Lord, the half of my goods I give to the poor; and if I have taken anything from any man by false accusation, I restore him fourfold."

9 And Jesus said to him, "This day is salvation come to this house, for he also is a son of Abraham. 10 For the Son of man is come to seek and to save that which was lost."

Background

Jericho was a lovely city called "The City of Palms," because the climate was tropical. It was watered by a magnificent spring that flowed to the nearby Jordan River. Herod the King had a palace there. He also built a citadel for its defense. There was a hippodrome for the people's entertainment.

Jesus is on his final journey to Jerusalem. He performed an extraordinary miracle on the way into Jericho when he healed the blind beggar Bartimaeus.

That miracle produced a loud and spontaneous response from a joyful Bartimaeus. This may have attracted even more people to the crowd around Jesus.

Transition: Who was this man named Zacchaeus that Jesus encountered in Jericho?

Zacchaeus was the chief tax collector of this wealthy district. His profession caused him to be hated by the people. His job allowed him the opportunity to cheat and steal through tax collection.

139

Though he was born and raised a Jew he was no longer considered a member of the Jewish religion. He was considered a great sinner.

He was a man without personal peace, without divine purpose, and without a place to belong. He was, as Jesus would describe him, a man who was lost.

He was small of stature. In this instance it would serve him well. It forced him to run ahead of the crowd and climb into a tree to see Jesus.

Jesus stopped beneath the tree and said to Zacchaeus, "Zacchaeus, come down immediately. I must stay at your house today."

The crowd was displeased and said, "He has gone to be a guest of a sinner."

Application

The outcome of the visit was transforming for Zacchaeus. Zacchaeus found what was missing in his life. He gained personal peace and a sense of divine purpose. Jesus restored him both to his rightful place in the Jewish nation as a descendent of Abraham, and to an eternal place in God's heavenly family.

Transition

What would you give for personal peace? Bookstores sell thousands of books with the word peace in the title for less than $25.00. Do you imagine you can buy peace for $25.00?

Illustration

Heath Ledger, the young 28 year old actor who died of a drug overdose, said he was so agitated and anxious that he couldn't sleep even one hour a night. He tried to buy personal peace through the use of at least six prescription narcotics. Sadly, they combined in his body to produce his death.

Hollywood has had a rash of young and beautiful people who have crashed because they sought peace in bottles of drugs or alcohol.

Application

The world can't give us peace. It can only take it away. Jesus is the one who can give us peace that comes and stays. Zacchaeus found peace through his faith in the Savior.

Question

How does Zacchaeus react to his new-found faith? He gave half his possessions to the poor. But, and this is so important to note, that was not the purpose of his life. The purpose of his life was to now serve Christ. For Zacchaeus, that meant giving away half of his possessions.

(Describe the scene as the servants of Zacchaeus take his food, possessions, and his money out to the crowd gathered outside the home.)

Illustration

I became a servant of Christ before I became a pastor. My wife and I were attending a city-wide crusade. The minister asked Christians in the crowd to make a commitment to serve Christ. We went forward and made that commitment. Some months later God called us to serve him in the ministry.

Application

The purpose of life is wonderfully simple. It's to serve our creator and redeemer, Jesus Christ. That service may take many forms over a lifetime.

Question

Do you have a divine purpose for your life? Have you made the commitment to serve Christ?

Jesus concluded this episode by saying, "For the Son of Man came to seek and to save what was lost."

He is describing Zacchaeus. Zacchaeus was lost but now he is found. He was born again spiritually into the family of God and was also returned physically to the covenant people of Abraham.

Summary

There were three great unmet needs in the life of Zacchaeus. He needed personal peace because he had none. He needed divine purpose because he had none. He needed a place to belong because he had lost his place.

All three needs were met in the person of Jesus Christ. Zacchaeus was so wise to go out of his way to see Jesus. More importantly, Jesus took time for Zacchaeus.

F. Visualization of the Solution

Illustration

John Newton was an Englishman who gained success by becoming the captain of his own ship. However, the ship he captained was a slave ship. He plied his trade from Africa to points around the world delivering his cargo of human slaves.

Once upon the high sea a mighty storm struck his ship. There was nothing captain or crew could do to save the ship. John Newton went to his cabin and began to pray and read the Bible.

When he came out of his cabin many hours later the storm on the sea had abated and the ship was still afloat. Another storm, the storm in his own heart, had also been made peaceful by the Prince of Peace.

He gave up the slave trade and took up the Bible. He became an Anglican minister. He was posted to London. There in London his experiences and his sermons helped fire the English abolition movement that led to the abolition of the slave trade.

I can give you John Newton's testimony with a few of his own words:

Amazing grace, how sweet the sound,
that saved a wretch like me!
I once was lost, but now am found,
was blind but now I see.

Conclusion to the Sermon

Sermon Summary

What do we see in both John Newton and Zacchaeus? We see men who were literally and figuratively adrift in life. Then Jesus found them and made them men of peace, purpose and place.

G. Call for Response

I believe there are three places where God wants us to be this morning. If we are in these three places then we are not lost. We are not drifting away from peace, purpose, and place.

What are these three places? They are places spoken of in God's word.

First, God wants us to be in the palm of his hand. In John 10:27-30, Jesus said:

27 My sheep hear my voice, and I know them, and they follow me. 28 And I give to them eternal life, and they shall never

143

perish; neither shall man pluck them out of my hand. 29 My Father, who gave them to me, is greater than all; and no one is able to snatch them out of my Father's hand. 30 I and my Father are one.

Second, God wants us to be with him in heaven. In John 14:2-3, Jesus said:

2 In my Father's house are any ⁺mansions; if it were not so, ⁺I would have told you. I go to prepare a place for you. 3 And if I go and prepare a place for you, I will come again and receive you to myself; that where I am, there you may be also.

Third, God wants us to be in his church. We read in Acts 2:41,

41 Then those who gladly received his word were baptized; and that day about three thousand souls were added to them.

H. Invitation

Would you prayerfully bow your heads for a moment? Now search your hearts. Are you truly in the place where you need to be? You don't have to answer.

But there in the solitude of your prayer, listen to God. You will want to ask him to find you. You will want to ask him to help you find your place.

Now will each of you give me your attention? I am going to step down to the front of the altar.

Invitation to Church Members

Will you come to the altar and these front pews this morning? Will you commit your life to serve the Lord? That is our eternal purpose. That is why we exist. Will you make that wonderful surrender this morning?

Invitation to Faith and Baptism

Dear friend, God wants to put you in the palm of his hand. Would you let this puny human hand of mine be a symbol this morning? Will you come give me your hand as a sign that you will trust Jesus Christ as your Lord and Savior?

Will you give me your hand as a sign that you will trust him to forgive your sins and someday take you to heaven? Come forward now. We will arrange for your baptism and church membership.

Invitation to Membership

I invite others of you to come forward to unite with this good church by transfer of membership. We will welcome and assist you in this decision.

I. Afterglow

Close the service with a prayer for those who have responded to the invitation.

Chapter 16
Sermon for Stewardship Sunday

Sermon Abstract

Title: Does God have a success plan for me?

Scripture: 2 Corinthians 9:6-8

Central Truths of the Scripture

God has a three-fold formula for Christians to follow for success.

1. Give generously according to God's spiritual law.

2. Give cheerfully out of love.

3. Trust God's grace to guide you to personal success.

Problem/Need to be Resolved

There are three questions we must all answer:

1. How can I provide for myself and my family?

2. How can I handle money so that I don't fail?

3. How can I know in my heart that I am doing the right things with my life?

Biblical Solution to the Problem/Need

The Apostle Paul gives us a three-fold answer to the three questions we must all answer:

1. How can I provide for myself and my family?

Answer: Give generously according to God's spiritual law.

2. How can I handle money so that I don't fail?

Answer: Give cheerfully out of love.

3. How can I know in my heart that I am doing the right things with my life?

Answer: Trust God's grace to guide you to personal success.

Sermon Purpose

To encourage Christians to accept God's plan of stewardship and follow it as a way of life

Introduction to the Sermon

A. Goodwill

On April 15, I mailed in my income tax return. I imagine I was one of millions of Americans who did so. You may be surprised to learn that it's always a time of thanksgiving for me. I give thanks that I was born an American. I also give thanks that early in my Christian experience I learned God's formula for success.

We Americans have been going through an economic rough patch. I have such a good word to share with you. It's the answer to the question, "Does God have a success formula for me?"

I want you to know that the answer I have for you I didn't get out of the *Wall Street Journal*, or the *New York Times*, or *Forbes Magazine*. The answer I have for you I found in the Bible, God's word.

There are some listening sheets available that have the scripture passage we are going to discuss. They will also allow you to jot down some of the thoughts we are going to share.

B. Pre-Invitation

At the end of our time with you today, I am going to ask you to make a decision that will help prepare you for whatever economic challenges may be coming at us.

I believe it is a decision that will truly bless your life. It will also bless those whom God has entrusted into your care. I am speaking of your loved ones, your family.

That's a big order, isn't it? That's why I would ask you to listen carefully.

We'll also extend an invitation to church membership. If you are looking for a church in which you can worship and serve our Lord, then we invite you to consider this church. We will welcome and assist you in the transfer of your membership.

The Bible says, "Today is the day of salvation." We invite you to make your public confession of faith today. We will be here at the altar to welcome and receive you. This church will arrange for your baptism and membership. Begin now to prayerfully consider this decision.

Transition: I am praying that God will help me communicate so clearly that you will understand completely the good news I want to share with you.

Please turn in your Bibles to 2 Corinthians 9:6-8

C. Attention

You and I both know that human communication can be a problem.

Humor

For instance, a New York woman was walking her Yorkshire terrier in Central Park. The woman walked by a disheveled man on a park bench eating a sandwich. The woman tried to ignore the decrepit character but the yorky was attracted to the sandwich. It stopped in front of the man and wouldn't budge.

"Would you like for me to throw the doggie a little?" the man asked.

The woman grudgingly relied, "Oh, I suppose so."

So the man reached down, released the leash and picked up the Yorky. Then he tossed it over a nearby hedge.

Looking at the stricken woman, he said, "If you will fetch the doggie, I will throw it a little more."

Transition

That was definitely a misunderstanding, wasn't it? It was a somewhat humorous misunderstanding unless you were the Yorky. I want you to clearly know and understand the good news that I have for you today.

Body of the Sermon

D. Problem/Need to be Resolved

The good news I have to share will answer the three questions we all face. I will repeat the questions.

1. How can I provide for myself and my family?

2. How can I handle money so that I don't fail?

3. How can I know in my heart that I am doing the right things with my life?

Don't you think those are pretty good questions to ask and answer? Don't you think those are pretty good questions for these difficult days?

So, what is the good news that answers these very basic questions?

Background

The good news answer is in the Bible, 2 Corinthians 9:6-8. First, let me set the stage before I read it to you.

The one giving the answers is the Apostle Paul. Immediately you can begin to have confidence in the answers, can't you?

Now here is the background of what Paul is saying. There is a famine in Palestine. The Christians in Jerusalem are really suffering. Paul is asking the Christians everywhere to give a generous gift to help them.

I can't really compare that time to our time, even though these are difficult times. You see, Christians were among the poorest of people in the Roman world. Many were slaves.

E. Biblical Solution to the Problem/Need

In asking these Christians for help Paul gives the answers to our questions:

1. How can I provide for myself and my family?

2. How can I handle money so that I don't fail?

3. How can I know in my heart that I am doing the right things with my life?

What does Paul say? Listen to 2 Corinthians 9:6-8:

6 But this I say, He that sows sparingly shall reap also sparingly; and he which sows bountifully shall reap also bountifully.

7 Every man according as he purposes in his heart, so let him give; not grudgingly, or of necessity: for God loves a cheerful giver.

8 And God is able to make all grace abound toward you; that you, always having all sufficiency in all things, may abound to every good work.

Solution Explained

Just as there are three questions for which we are seeking answers, Paul has three answers. Two of the answers pertain to what we must do. The third answer tells us what God will do.

The first question is: How can I provide for myself and my family?

Paul's answer is: Give generously according to God's spiritual law.

The second question is: How can I handle money so that I don't fail?

Paul's answer is: Give cheerfully out of love.

The third question is: How can I know in my heart that I am doing the right things with my life?

Paul's answer is: Trust God's grace to guide you to personal success.

Transition

Let's quickly examine each answer that God gives to our questions. The answers will reveal how will God keep us from failing the financial challenges that are ahead of us?

First Question: How can I provide for myself and my family?

Paul's answer is: Give generously according to God's spiritual law.

The Bible simply says that we are to follow God's spiritual law of giving, just as the farmer follows God's natural law of sowing.

6 Remember this: Whoever sows sparingly will also reap sparingly, and whoever sows generously will also reap generously.

Fortunately for us God's spiritual law of giving and receiving is very straightforward. It's a contract between us and God. Here it is in a nutshell from Malachi 3:10-12.

10 Bring all the tithes into the storehouse, that there may be meat in my house, and prove me now herewith says the Lord of hosts, if I will not open you the windows of heaven, and pour you out a blessing, that there shall not be room enough to receive it.

11 And I will rebuke the devourer for your sakes, and he shall not destroy the fruits of your ground; neither shall your vine cast her fruit before the time in the field, says the Lord of hosts.

12 And all nations shall call you blessed: for you shall be a delightsome land, says the Lord of hosts.

What was the first of our questions? How can I provide for myself and my family?

Application: God says bring the tithe to the Church (Storehouse). Then God says he will spring into action and bless. You will be so blessed that even strangers (all the nations) can't help but notice how blessed you are.

What can you expect to happen if you obey this spiritual law? May I give you an example?

Illustration

Shortly after becoming a Christian I learned about God's spiritual law of giving and receiving. So I began to tithe my little weekly salary of $18.00 a week. This was my pay for working at a diner after school.

I gave $2.00 each week. I haven't stopped giving the tithe and above the tithe ever since that first job.

In 1965, Parkview Baptist Church asked me to be their pastor. I agreed. There was one condition. They asked me to join the SBC retirement program. It cost $33.34 a month, or $400 a year. It was called Plan A. It would provide enough money to bury me and give my wife a little annuity. I agreed and started the retirement program.

I stayed in the program until 1982. That's when the SBC changed over into a 403B type of retirement program. They called it Plan B. I had paid about $6800 into Plan A.

I forgot all about Plan A. I figured I had gotten my money's worth in the protection it had promised to my family.

Then in 1995, a friend asked me what I had in Plan A.

I actually said, "What Plan A?"

He said it was the old retirement plan. I said I figured I had nothing in it. He insisted that there was something in it and suggested I write and find out how much was in the old plan.

153

I wrote the Annuity Board a letter asking what I had in Plan A. The Board sent a letter informing me that I had $57,000 in Plan A. After my wife had revived me we gave thanks to God.

Then a year later I wrote and asked again what I had in Plan A. The Annuity Board wrote back that I now had $63,000 in Plan A.

I became eligible to draw funds from Plan A in 1997. The final payment was made in October 2009. Over the 12 years of payout I had received more than $110,000. I received all of that money from the Plan I had forgotten about. I used the money to pay off my home, buy a decent car, and invest in another retirement program.

Summary

Now what was the question? How can I provide for myself and my family? What was Paul's answer? Give with generosity according to God's spiritual law.

Application

I know God's law of giving and receiving works because it has worked in my life. But being a Baptist pastor, I have seen it work in hundreds of Christian families.

Transition

Now let's see what Paul has to say about the second of our questions:

2. Second Question: How can I handle my money so that I don't fail?

Biblical Solution to the Second Question: How can I handle my money so that I don't fail?

Paul's answer: Give cheerfully out of love.

154

Listen to the scripture:

7 Each man should give what he has decided in his heart to give, not reluctantly or under compulsion, for God loves a cheerful giver.

The Bible tells us in I Timothy 6:10, that the love of money is the root of all evil. The wrong attitude toward money will lead us away from God. The right attitude toward money is like having a compass always pointing true north. It keeps us from losing our way concerning money.

God wants us to decide to give. Make no mistake about that. But, he wants us to do so with joy. He doesn't want us to do it out of necessity, as though we were paying a bill.

There ought to be joy in our giving. Giving is an act of worship. Giving is really an act of love. We are showing our love for God.

Question

What would happen if you decided to give and to do so out of your love for God?

Illustration

When I was pastor in Duncan, Oklahoma, the church had a part-time music director. He also worked for the Halliburton Company. His wife played the church organ.

We were getting ready for our annual stewardship drive and I asked for volunteers to give tithing testimonies. The music director immediately volunteered.

He told me, "I believe in tithing."

So I asked, "Why?"

He told me the story of how he had begun to tithe. He said he and his wife realized they needed to tithe so that made a commitment to do so. He figured his annual salary, divided by 52, and that is what he gave.

But, he said, "I worked overtime many weeks. I just ignored the extra money and kept on giving the weekly amount I had figured. Then, my gall bladder went bad. I had the radical surgery and was off work for about 6 weeks."

He continued, "At the end of the year, I was figuring my taxes. I always itemize. Suddenly, it jumped out at me. The cost of my gall bladder surgery was, to the dollar, the exact amount of what my tithe should have been if I had added in my overtime."

"Do you mean you think God collected your unpaid tithe by giving you a bad gall bladder?" I asked.

"No," he said, "that's too complicated for my poor brain. What I think is this. I made an agreement with God and then broke my part. God sent me a message?"

"And what was the message," I asked?

He replied, "God said to me, do you really want to do this? Do you want me involved in your finances? Make up your mind."

He went on, "I got serious about my giving. And God has been so good to us. Let me tell the folks what a joy it is to give."

When he retired from Halliburton, he and his wife moved to a cabin on Lake Texoma. That was his dream and he got it.

Application

Paul is teaching us that there is a way to handle money so that we don't fail at it. He is telling us to handle it as God teaches. We are to be generous in our giving, and to do so cheerfully.

Review: We are looking at God's answer to our questions:

1. How can I provide for myself and my family?

2. How can I handle money so that I don't fail?

3. How can I know in my heart that I am doing the right things with my life?

Transition

We now come to the third, and I think the most important answer to our question: How can I know in my heart that I am doing the right things with my life?

3. Biblical Answer to the Third Question: How can I know in my heart that I am doing the right things with my life?

Paul's answer: Trust God's grace to guide us to personal success.

Listen again to what the scripture says:

8 And God is able to make all grace abound to you, so that in all things at all times; having all that you need, you will abound in every good work.

Do you see it?

First, you give with generosity according to God's spiritual law.

Second, you give cheerfully, out of love for God.

Application

And then what happens? God supplies all your needs. God guides you throughout your life. God brings you home at the end of life's long journey, content and complete. Isn't that what the verse says? Wow!

F. Visualization of the Biblical Solution

Have you ever been hospitalized? Were you fortunate enough to have a remarkable nurse to care for you? Then, you can thank Florence Nightingale because she is the one who brought modern nursing into being.

She was an English woman, born of an aristocratic family in 1820. She lived into the early part of the 20th century. She turned her back on an easy upper class existence to go into nursing.

During the Crimean campaign by English military forces, Florence Nightingale gained the nickname, "The Lady with the Lamp," derived from a phrase in a report in the "London Times."

The *Times* wrote:

She is a ministering angel without any exaggeration in these hospitals, and as her slender form glides quietly along each corridor, every poor fellow's face softens with gratitude at the sight of her.

When all the medical officers have retired for the night and silence and darkness have settled down upon those miles of prostrate sick, she may be observed alone, with a little lamp in her hand, making her solitary rounds.

A passage from Florence Nightingale's personal diary will help us understand this remarkable woman. At age thirty she wrote in her diary:

I am thirty years of age, the age at which Christ began His mission. No more childish things, no more vain things. Now, Lord, let me think only of thy will.

Years later, near the end of her heroic life, she was asked for her life's secret.

She replied, "I can only give one explanation. That is, I have kept nothing back from God."

Summary

Florence Nightingale kept nothing back from the Lord. The whole world has been blessed by her life. She is an example to us that if we do our part, God will do his. We will fulfill our purpose in life. God will see to it.

Application

Again, what happens when we give with generosity to God's work? What happens when we give joyfully, out of our love for Him?

God supplies all our needs. God guides us throughout our life. God brings us home at the end of life's long journey, content and complete. That's what God did with and for Florence Nightingale. I will say it again, wow!

Conclusion to the Sermon

Summary of Sermon

Now, I want to ask you, "What answers are you going to give to those three questions that we all face?"

1. **How can I provide for myself and my family?**

2. **How can I handle money so that I don't fail?**

3. **How can I know in my heart that I am doing the right things with my life?**

We have seen God's answers through Paul's admonition to Christians just like us. He said, if I may paraphrase:

1. Give generously according to God's spiritual law.

2. Give cheerfully out of love for Christ.

3. Trust God's grace to guide you to personal success.

Transition

Remember how we began this message? I said that at the end of it I would ask you to make a decision that would prepare you for whatever economic challenges might come your way.

I said that I thought it would be a decision that would truly bless your life, and bless those whom God has entrusted into your care.

Quote

I am reminded of what Joshua said to the Israelites. He said: "Choose you this day who you will serve. As for me and my house, we will serve the Lord."

G. Call for Response

Today, we can choose to go it alone through these hard times. We can tell God to butt out and stay out of our financial lives. Or we can choose to ask God to partner with us, especially in the area of our finances.

H. Invitation

Invitation to the Church family

I am now going to ask you to take a moment to pray about the decision God would have you to make.

Then prayerfully check the appropriate statements, under D, "My Decision," on the listening sheet. You can check more than one statement. Fold the sheet and come place it on the altar as we sing the invitation hymn.

Invitation to Faith and Baptism

May I give a special encouragement to those who are not yet part of this church family? This is a good Sunday to begin your walk of faith with Jesus, our Lord. He is here today to forgive you for all the failures of the past, to forgive your sins, to save you for all eternity.

And this is so important, to walk with you through the unknown challenges that are ahead. Please come to me. We will receive you and arrange for your baptism and membership.

Invitation to Church Membership

Also, may I say a word of encouragement to those who are considering this church for your spiritual home? Please come to me that I may also receive you and assist you.

I. Afterglow

Conclude the service with the "Doxology."

FYI: Listening sheet and suggested follow up are on the next two pages.

LISTENING SHEET

A. Scripture: 2 Corinthians 9:6-8

B. What are the three questions we must answer?

1. _____.

2. _____.

3. _____.

C. What are God's answers to the three questions?

1. _____.

2. _____.

3. _____.

D. My Decision:

___I want to confess Christ and receive baptism.

___I want to move my membership into this loving church.

___I will give joyfully with love to God.

___I will give the tithe joyfully with love to God.

___I will give the tithe and an offering joyfully with love to God.

My Signature: _____

Follow up

This sermon might be used to launch a stewardship emphasis. It was used in this manner at Northeast Baptist Church, Norman, Oklahoma.

The idea of the listening sheet was borrowed from Dr. Ed Sasnett, pastor of Northeast. Dr. Sasnett conducts a stewardship emphasis each year.

He has a unique approach. He doesn't ask members to pledge dollar amounts. Instead, he asks them to give on a regular basis.

He keeps a record of the percentages of each level of commitment. He challenges the members to increase the percentages each year. This approach has proven very successful.

Pastor, if you're interested in this approach, I have Dr. Sasnett's permission to use his name and Church. You can find Northeast Baptist Church, Norman, Oklahoma, on the internet. Ed will respond to your inquiries.

Chapter 17
Sermon for Fall Festival Sunday

Sermon Abstract

Title: Trick or treat?

Scripture: Luke 23:39-46

Central Truths of Passage

1. The thief understood the human condition of being lost.

2. He understood who Jesus was.

3. He understood the human response required.

4. He understood that his redemption was amazing, beyond words.

The Problem/Need in the Story

A common thief was dying on a cross. He realized that he had lived a wasted life. Was there any redemption for such a hopeless case? He is a picture of all those who are living without God's love and redemption.

The Solution in the Story

Much to the amazement of the thief he discovered that the central cross was occupied by Jesus, the promised Messiah. At the very time when others were doubting Jesus this man decided to put his faith in the Lord.

It's an example of unparalleled faith for such a time and circumstance. It's also an answer to anyone who asks. "Can I be saved?"

Sermon Purpose

To encourage listener to follow the example of the thief on the cross and look to the Lord Jesus for salvation

Introduction to the Sermon

A. Goodwill

This is my favorite time of year. First, the weather is my favorite. Second, it has three of my favorite holidays; beginning with Halloween, then Thanksgiving, and finally the best of all holidays, Christmas.

As you may observe by the title of the sermon, we are going to talk about Halloween's trick or treat, but with a biblical twist.

B. Pre-Invitation

There will be an invitation at the conclusion of the message this morning. I will be at the front of the sanctuary to welcome and assist those of you who desire to unite with this church by transfer of membership.

Some may want to use this occasion to make a public confession of faith in our Lord Jesus Christ. We will receive you and arrange for your baptism.

Now I know that there are many reasons why we are here today. God has promised to be among us. Would each be open to hear His voice? Thank you.

C. Attention

When my children were growing up we always enjoyed the Charlie Brown Halloween TV special. Charlie Brown is the little round headed boy who has a hard time getting it right.

Lucy never lets him kick the football. He can't seem to charm the little red-headed girl. And infatuated Peppermint Pattie won't leave him alone.

In the television special the children assemble under the street lamp, dressed in their Halloween costumes, to begin the night of trick-or-treating. You immediately know which child is Charlie Brown.

Several of the children are dressed up like ghosts. Charlie is the one whose sheet looks like the coat of a Dalmatian puppy. There are a multitude of eye holes cut into the sheet.

The children began their happy trek from house to house. Occasionally they stop under the street lamps to check their sacks for goodies. Some have candy bars. Some have apples and oranges. Some have tootsie pops and gum. But when Charlie Brown looks into his sack, he says, "I've got rocks."

The children go from house to house. The treasures of candy and fruit accumulate. But each time they stop to check their sacks Charlie Brown says, "All I have are rocks."

Transition

We're going to talk about a man who came to the end of his life and looked into his sack of accumulated treasures and found rocks. There was no faith there. There was no hope there. The love of God was not there. We read his story in Luke 23:39-46.

Body of the Sermon

Read and Discuss the Scripture Passage

39 And one of the malefactors which were hanged blasphemed him, saying, if you be Christ, save yourself and us.

40 But the other answering rebuked him, saying, don't you fear God, seeing you are in the same condemnation? 41 And we indeed justly; for we receive the due reward of our deeds: but this man has done nothing amiss.

This thief was actually committing blasphemy by mocking Jesus. The fact that Jesus was sharing a common death convinced him that Jesus was a fraud.

Other translations say the thief abused or mocked him. Blasphemy is a religious term. It was the crime the Sanhedrin accused Jesus of committing because he claimed to be the Messiah, the Son of God. Blasphemy is attributing the things of God to Satan (evil), or the things of Satan (evil) to God.

The term, "Christ," is the New Testament equivalent of the Old Testament "Messiah."

42 And he said to Jesus, Lord; remember me when you come into you kingdom. 43 And Jesus said to him, Verily I say to you, To day shall you be with me in paradise.

The believing thief recognized that death was not the end of life. There was eternity and God beyond the grave. The word, paradise (pardes), is a Persian word. It was the king's garden.

It came to mean a world of rest, peace and happiness beyond the grave. It is used synonymously for heaven in 2 Corinthians 12:4, and Revelation 2:7.

44 And it was about the sixth hour, and there was darkness over all the earth until the ninth hour. 45 And the sun was darkened, and the veil of the temple was rent in the midst.

46 And when Jesus had cried with a loud voice, he said, Father, into your hands I commend my spirit: and having said thus, he gave up the ghost.

Explain the Background of the Story

At 9:00am that Friday morning, Jesus was crucified between two thieves. During the morning hours he forgave his persecutors saying,

"Father, forgive them. They do not know what they are doing."

Later, he gave the care of his mother into the hands of John the Apostle saying,

"Woman, behold your son. Behold your mother."

One thief abused him but the other recognized him as the Christ. He requested of Jesus,

"Lord, remember me when you come into your kingdom?"

Jesus answered,

"Assuredly I say to you, today you shall be with me in Paradise."

Now it was noon. Darkness fell upon the earth. Out of the darkness Jesus cried out,

"I thirst."

A sponge with water and vinegar was raised to his lips. And then,

"My God, my God, why have you forsaken me?"

This is the opening line of psalm 22, the great Messianic Psalm. David wrote prophetically,

My God, My God, why have you forsaken me? Why are you so] far from helping me, And from the words of my groaning?

Toward 3:00pm in the afternoon, Jesus said,

"It is finished."

Then at about 3:00pm, Jesus said,

"Father, into your hands I commit my spirit."

Having said this, he breathed his last breath. John wrote so gently, "He bowed his head and died."

Summary

Jesus had been crucified with a common thief on his left and right. We don't know whether the man we are talking about was on the left or the right. It doesn't really matter. What matters is that the man was dying.

When he looked into the bag of life's treasures he found only rocks. We know this because the man reprimands the other thief for mocking and railing against Jesus.

He said:

40 Do you not even fear God, seeing you are under the same condemnation? 41 And we indeed justly, for we receive the due reward of our deeds; but this Man has done nothing wrong.

D. The Problem in the Story

The crisis of the thief on the cross offers us an analogy of the human situation for each of us this morning.

First, the thief faced in only one direction and that direction was death and eternity.

Second, he couldn't go back to undo his circumstances. All the regret in the world wouldn't change the fact of his sins, or any act of sin. Nor can any of us undo the deeds of our lives.

Third, he could make no plans of his own. His future lay in the hands of God. So it is with all of us. Our plans will dwindle into insignificance as death and eternity approach. We too, will be in the hands of God.

Transition

The crucifixion caused the thief to consider life. Sadly it took an agonizing execution to force this man to face up to the failure of his life.

E. Solution to the Problem in the Story

1. First, he understood the human condition of being lost.

While the other thief railed against Jesus to save them from this horrible death, he accepted his circumstances and acknowledged his guilt.

When we find ourselves in difficulties: a crushed car, a foxhole, a funeral, a failed marriage, or a debilitating illness, we also can choose to rail against heaven; or we can cast ourselves upon the mercy of heaven.

2. Second, he understood who Jesus was.

The crucifixion caused the thief to consider death. He was unprepared for death. When he looked into his bag containing the treasures of his life he didn't find faith. He didn't find hope or the love of God in the bag.

And then to his amazement he looked at the man on the central cross and recognized the Son of God.

a. Jesus is unequaled in consecration. His love for us sent him to the cross. He gave his life for us. The Bible says,

> *For the son of man is come to seek and to save that which was lost.* Luke 19:10

> But none of the ransomed ever knew
> How deep were the waters crossed,
> Nor how dark was the night that the Lord passed through
> Ere he found his sheep that was lost.

b. Jesus is unequaled in saving power. Again, the Bible says,

> *Neither is there salvation in any other: for there is none other name under heaven given among men, whereby we must be saved.* Acts 4:12

3. Third, he understood the human response required.

a. He confessed Jesus as king when others mocked his kingship.

b. He wanted to be part of a spiritual kingdom others could not understand.

c. He recognized Christ's victory over death when others thought death had defeated him.

d. He believed in Christ as the promised Savior when others crucified him for the claim.

171

e. He recognized his need of forgiveness and not rescue, and sought that. Then he said to Jesus, *"Lord, remember me when you come into your kingdom."* (42)

4. Fourth, he understood his redemption was amazing, beyond words.

And Jesus said to him, Assuredly, I say to you, today you will be with me in Paradise. (43)

The thief grew quiet. There are no other utterances recorded. I used to wonder why. Then I read in the Holy Scriptures that God gives us a joy unspeakable.

Think of what Jesus did for this man. Imagine how you would feel if he had done it for you. What would you say to the Lord? What could you say to him? Wouldn't you also grow silent in wonder and joy!

Just now take a look into your bag of treats. Do you have faith in that bag? Do you have hope in that bag? Do you have the love of God in that bag?

If these treasures are not there, then I pray that you won't wait until the hour of your death. That may be too late. You may not be able to call upon the Lord. You might not even know how to call upon the Lord.

Illustration

There is an old story about a doughboy in WWI. The soldier is advancing across a shell cratered battlefield. Shells begin to fall all around him. He jumps into a crater and hugs the earth.

Then his eyes see something shinny in the wall of the crater. He grasps it and pulls it out of the earth. He stares at it and realizes that it's a crucifix.

At that same moment a chaplain dives into the same crater. The American doughboy recognizes the insignias on the chaplain's shirt.

He holds out the crucifix to the chaplain and says, "How do you make this thing work?"

F. Visualization of the Solution

I want to close our time together by telling you about another man who looked into his bag of life's treasures and found only rocks. Jesus told his story.

Illustration

It is the story of the prodigal son. That son asked his father for his inheritance and the father gave it to him. He took it and went into a far country where he wasted it on riotous living.

He became so destitute that he hired out to feed pigs. He was so hungry he wanted to eat what the hogs were eating. At that moment of desperation, he came to himself.

He realized that the servants in his father's house had it better than he did. He resolved to go back to his father, not as his son, but as a destitute and morally bankrupt man. He would ask his father to take him back as a servant.

When he returned the father took him back. But he didn't take him back as a servant. No, the father took him back as the son that was lost and is now found. He celebrated his return with a ring, a robe and a kiss. The father gave a banquet in honor of the son who had been returned to him.

Transition

Jesus told that story to illustrate the heart of God toward those of us who look into the bag of life's treasures and find the bag is empty of faith, hope, and the love of God.

Conclusion to the Sermon

Sermon Summary

Let's review what we've learned. The thief on the cross realized he was a sinner condemned and justly so. He acknowledged that his troubles were of his own making, and that he was getting what he deserved. Then wonder of wonders, he discovered the Messiah, Jesus the son of God, crucified on a cross next to him. Under these difficult circumstances he expressed a most amazing faith in Jesus.

1. The thief confessed Jesus as king when others mocked his kingship.

2. He wanted to be part of a spiritual kingdom others could not understand.

3. The thief recognized Christ's victory over death when others thought death had defeated him.

4. He believed in Christ as the promised Savior when others crucified him for the claim.

5. The man recognized his need of forgiveness and not rescue, and sought that.

And that very day, before the evening came, that dying thief was walking with Jesus in the garden of Paradise.

G. Call for Response

I believe God would have every one of us take an honest look into the bag of life's treasures that we have accumulated. Is there faith in the bag? Is there heavenly hope in your bag of life's treasures? What about love? Do you have the saving, protecting, transforming love of God in there?

H. Invitation

Invitation to Faith and Baptism

Please bow your heads for just a moment. If you know you have trusted Jesus and are sure you are going to heaven, please raise your hand. Thank you. Some did not raise their hands.

May I ask that everyone look at me for a just a moment. I have good news for you this morning.

The good news is that Jesus Christ has done all that is necessary to give each of us life after death, and to take us to heaven.

You don't have to earn or deserve heaven. Thank goodness, because none of could earn or deserve heaven anyway. Heaven is a gift that God gives to you when you trust Jesus as your Savior and Lord.

Again, would all bow in prayer for just a moment? Please whisper this prayer after me there at your seats.

"Heavenly Father, I want to thank you for sending Jesus to die on that cruel cross for my sins. Please forgive me for my sinfulness and failures. I confess that Jesus is the Savior and Lord. I trust him to save me today, tomorrow and forever. Amen."

Now we are all going to stand. I will step down to the front. I want to invite you to come to me and give me your hand as a sign that you were sincere in your prayer. This church will joyfully receive you and arrange for your baptism.

Invitation to Church Membership

We also extend an invitation to those who may be seeking a church family to worship with, serve with, and pray with. This good church will welcome you and be helpful in securing the transfer of your membership.

I. Afterglow

Now the Lord of peace himself give to you peace at all times in all ways. And may the Lord be with all of you. Amen.
2 Thessalonians 3:16

Chapter 18
Sermon for Thanksgiving Sunday

Sermon Abstract

Title: Will Thanksgiving heal a hurting heart?

Scripture: Luke 17:11-19

Central Truth of the Scripture Passage

The Samaritan who gave thanks to God received the gift of wholeness from the hand of Christ. There is a pattern in this story that we can follow to find wholeness.

Problem/Need to be Resolved

Many people have troubled hearts and lives at this Thanksgiving season. They may be troubled by a personal problem. It may be an illness. It may be regret. Perhaps they are troubled by a family problem. Hearts may not be at peace.

Where can they find help?

Biblical Solution to the Problem/Need

The story of the Samaritan leper offers a recipe of help to those who are hurting this Thanksgiving season:

First, like the leper, we can call out to the Lord, "Have mercy on us. Please have mercy!"

Second, like the leper, we can praise the lord. We can acknowledge that the good that has happened to us has come from the hand of God through Christ.

Third, we can give thanks to the Lord. We can replace anger, or bitterness, or rebellion, or hopelessness, or disappointment, with a thankful mind and spirit.

Fourth, we can cast all our cares upon him for he cares for us. We can go forth from this place renewed and whole again.

Sermon Purpose

To encourage listeners to turn to Christ, even as the Samaritan leper did, to find healing and wholeness

Introduction to the Sermon

A. Goodwill

B. Pre-Invitation

There will be an invitation at the conclusion of the message this morning. I will be at the front of the sanctuary to welcome and assist those of you who desire to unite with this church by transfer of membership.

Some may want to use this occasion to make a public confession of faith in our Lord Jesus Christ. We will receive you and arrange for your baptism.

Now I know that there are many reasons why we are here today. God has promised to be among us. Would each be open to hear His voice? Thank you.

C. Attention

I believe we are living in troubling times this Thanksgiving season. What are some of the kinds of trouble people may be having just now. We may be troubled by finances or a personal problem. It may be an illness. It may be regret. Perhaps we are troubled by a family difficulty. At this Thanksgiving season not all hearts are at peace.

If that's your case, I have a wonderful insight from God's word. The act of thanksgiving may have the power to bring healing balm to troubled hearts. The act of thanksgiving may be the way to peace and joy in this Thanksgiving season.

Body of the Sermon

D. Problem/Need to be Resolved

Life has a way of bringing unwanted troubles to our door. These troubles can steal away our joy and peace. These troubles can put life under great stress.

Sometimes we show the world a brave face. But deep in our hearts there is pain and sorrow.

Transition

We'll see God's answer for hurting hearts in a story found in the New Testament. Turn to the Gospel of Luke 17:11-19:

Background

Ten tribes to the north revolted against Solomon's son Rehoboam in 932-931 B.C. A new nation was formed and was called Israel. Its capital city was Samaria and was ruled by Jeroboam. He wasn't a descendant of King David. The king created a rival temple to keep the people from going down to Jerusalem.

The nation fell to Assyria in 722 B.C. Many of the people were deported. People of other nations were imported and settled in Israel. They became a mixed race and were called Samaritans.

In the time of Rome, Israel was divided into three provinces; Galilee, Samaria, and Judah.

Jesus is journeying from Galilee. He's traveling along the border of Samaria on the way to Judah. It will be his last trip to the Holy City of Jerusalem. He is destined to be crucified there.

179

Read the Scripture Passage: Luke 17:11-19

11 It came to pass, as he went to Jerusalem that he passed through the midst of Samaria and Galilee. 12 And as he entered into a certain village, there met him ten men that were lepers, which stood afar off: 13 and they lifted up their voices, and said, Jesus, Master, have mercy on us.

14 And when he saw them, he said to them, Go show yourselves unto the priests. And it came to pass, that, as they went, they were cleansed.

15 And one of them, when he saw that he was healed, turned back, and with a loud voice glorified God, 16 and fell down on his face at his feet, giving him thanks: and he was a Samaritan.

17 And Jesus answering said, was there not ten cleansed? But where are the nine? 18 There are not found that returned to give glory to God, save this stranger.

19 And he said to him, Arise, go your way: your faith has made you whole.

Discussion of the Scripture Passage

Jesus and his disciples were making a trip to Jerusalem. It was his final journey. It will end with his death by crucifixion at the hands of Roman soldiers.

As they reach the border between Galilee and Samaria, ten men who have leprosy recognize Jesus. The lepers call out to Jesus for mercy.

Consider the horrible condition of these ten lepers. They have a dreadful disease. They are cut off from society and family. They were penniless and reduced to begging. They had little or no hope that their condition could improve.

I want to give them credit for acting wisely in this situation. They could have begged for food. If so, it would have been consumed by evening.

They could have begged for money. If so, it would have been spent soon enough. They wisely asked Jesus for mercy.

Jesus was moved with compassion. He told them to go show themselves to the priest.

There are two things to note about this:

First, when a leper considered that he was healed of the disease he had to go to the priest for confirmation before he could return to society. It was a lengthy process that could take days before he was fully restored to the community.

Second, Jesus healed in different ways. Previously he had healed a leper with his touch. This time the lepers had to obey the command to go to the priest. As they were going they were healed of the disease.

These men constitute a chorus of the miserable. They lifted their voices as one, seeking deliverance from the awfulness that existence had become for them.

I'm sure Jesus also lifted his voice to give them a way to rid themselves of their horrid condition.

Visualize the Scene

Imagine for the audience what the scene might have been like as the lepers talked over what Jesus had said to them.

"I'm not going. Religion has never helped me."

"I'm not going. He didn't do what I expected."

"I'm not going. I can't stand being disappointed again."

181

"I knew we should have asked for money."

One of them, perhaps the one who acted as their leader, might have said, "Really. How much religion have you ever tried?"

And to another of the complaints he may have answered, "Really. Do you know his business better than he does? When did you heal or help anybody? We know what's said about him. He cares for and helps even the worst and lowest of men."

Perhaps to the one who was worrying about being disappointed he might have said, "Disappointment is something we all know about. Everything about us is a vast disappointment. What would one more disappointment be to the likes of us? Besides, what if it works?"

The ten lepers started for the priest. As they were going they realized that they had been healed. One of the lepers, and only one, turned back to thank Jesus for the healing. The one who returned was a Samaritan.

Jesus was astonished that only one, and that one a Samaritan, had turned back to thank him for this remarkable miracle.

That brings us to verse nineteen. The Samaritan returned glorifying God in a loud voice. This means he was specifically giving God credit for his healing.

Visualize the Scene

I can see him running back to Jesus and the disciples. I can hear him shouting, "I'm healed. Praise God! Praise God, I'm healed. Do you hear me, I'm healed! Thank God, praise God!"

Perhaps some of the disciples were startled or even frightened.

The Samaritan threw himself to the ground at the feet of Jesus.

Jesus said to him, "Rise and go; your faith has made you well."

It's important for us to note that Jesus used a different word than that which is normally used for healing. There's a world of difference between the two words. The usual word for healing means the removal of a physical condition that was troubling the individual; i.e., conditions such as blindness, lameness, or leprosy.

The word Jesus used to describe the condition of the healed leper was the word for wholeness.

E. Biblical Solution to the Problem/Need

Do you see it? Ten lepers went to see the priest. As they were going they were healed of the leprosy. Only one of them, a Samaritan, turned back. He fell at the feet of Jesus and gave thanks.

When he got to his feet he had not only experienced the healing of the body, but he had also experienced the healing of the heart. He had been made whole. It had happened as he gave thanks.

Transition

What if we followed the example of the grateful Samaritan? Might we find wholeness? Might we find healing for our hurting hearts? Might we find the way to thankfulness instead of sadness this Thanksgiving?

F. Visualization of the Solution

May I share with you a Bible story with which we're all familiar? It illustrates what might happen when we give thanks to God in difficult circumstances.

It's the story of Jonah. Jonah was God's prophet. God spoke to Jonah and commissioned him to go the Gentile city of Nineveh. He was to proclaim a message or repentance and judgment.

You know what happened. Jonah didn't want to go. So he ran in the opposite direction. He went down to Joppa. He went down to Tarshish. He went down into a ship. The ship encountered a storm. Jonah confessed to being the cause of God's anger and asked the sailor's to throw him overboard. They finally consented and tossed him over.

Jonah went down into the sea. Then a large fish swallowed him and he went down into the belly of the fish. Then the fish went down to the bottom of the sea.

There in the darkness, in the belly of the fish, at the bottom of the sea, Jonah did a most unusual thing. He began to give thanks to God.

Read: Jonah 2:9-10

9 But I will sacrifice to you with the voice of thanksgiving; I will pay that that I have vowed. Salvation is of the Lord.

10 And the Lord spoke to the fish, and it vomited out Jonah upon the dry land.

"Why did Jonah give thanks" you ask? Because Jonah recognized that God had saved him. Even in the midst of his circumstances he recognized the hand of God.

What would have happened if Jonah hadn't responded to his desperate situation with thanksgiving? I will tell you. He would have ended up as fish food. And he would have gone into eternity as an angry and rebellious prophet, disobeying the very God who would be his judge.

We know the rest of the story. God's response to Jonah's act of thanksgiving was to deliver Jonah to dry land. Then Jonah turned toward Nineveh. He proclaimed God's message. The whole city of Nineveh repented and was saved from destruction.

Summary

This all happened because a willful, rebellious prophet started giving thanks to God. He was delivered and a whole city was saved. There is power in thanksgiving.

Scripture Quote: Philippians 4:6-7

> *6 Be anxious about nothing; but in everything by prayer and supplication with thanksgiving let your requests be made known unto God. 7 And the peace of God, which passes all understanding, shall keep your hearts and minds through Christ Jesus.*

Application

From the story of Jonah we have learned that thanksgiving is a good way for a rebellious and backslidden man to begin again to obey and serve the Lord. From the story of the grateful Samaritan leper we have learned the steps to wholeness.

Conclusion to the Sermon

Sermon Summary

Some of us come to the Thanksgiving season with troubled lives and hurting hearts. The story of the healed leper presents us with a better way to observe Thanksgiving.

The story of Jonah illustrates that thanksgiving is a good place to begin when we need God's help to climb out of a desperate situation.

G. Call for Response

We can also do what the Samaritan Leper did. Let's review again the steps followed by the grateful Samaritan in the Bible passage.

First, like the leper, we can call out to the Lord, "Have mercy on us. Please have mercy!"

Second, like the leper, we can praise the lord. We can acknowledge that the good that has happened to us in our lives has come from the hand of God through Christ.

Third, we can start giving thanks in this very moment. We can replace anger, or bitterness, or rebellion, or hopelessness, or disappointment, with a thankful mind and spirit.

Fourth, we can cast all our cares upon him for he cares for us. We can go forth from this place renewed and whole again.

H. Invitation

Invitation to the Church

I want to encourage you to come kneel, sit or stand at the altar. Follow the steps of the Samaritan and come to the altar to praise and give thanks to God.

Don't leave until God touches your heart and makes you know he is with you.

Then return with him to your seats. This is how we can have peace and joy. Come and give thanks to God!

Invitation to Faith and Baptism

Invite the unsaved to choose this Sunday morning to be made whole through the saving faith of Jesus Christ.

I. Afterglow

Peace I leave with you, my peace I give to you; not as the world gives do I give to you. Let not your heart be troubled, neither let it be afraid.
John 14:27

Chapter 19
Sermon for Christmas Eve

Sermon Abstract

Title: What will you do in remembrance of him?

Scripture: Matthew 26:17-30

Central Truth of the Passage

The joy of Christmas is to know and love Jesus Christ. It's he who came to be Savior and Lord for a lost and dying world.

Problem/Need to be Resolved

Christmas is supposed to be a time of hope, joy and peace. But what if one doesn't have the joy of Christmas? Is there a way to find it again?

Biblical Solution to the Problem/Need

The first Christmas was a time of fear and foreboding. The birth of Jesus Christ brought hope, peace, and joy, to the many who heard the good news. The story of the birth of the Savior can still drive out fear and replace it with hope, peace and joy.

Sermon Purpose

To encourage listeners to commit themselves to the saving grace of Jesus Christ and thereby experience the joy of Christmas.

Introduction to the Sermon

A. Goodwill

Welcome! Are you enjoying the lights and decorations of the Christmas season? Isn't the church warm and welcoming for this candlelight service?

Humor

I understand that our nation's capital is also beautifully decorated with many trees and lights. However, this year the capitol will not have a Nativity scene. It isn't because of religious reasons. I understand they couldn't find three wise men.

B. Pre-Invitation

There will be a silent invitation at the conclusion of the communion service. Please pass the communion response slips that are located at the ends of the pews. Everyone will want one. (Slips can also be placed in the service bulletin.)

During the invitation hymn the congregation will be invited to bring the communion response slips to the communion table.

Guests are also invited to participate.

Our prayer is that some attending tonight will use this opportunity to follow Christ and become members of this congregation. We will happily arrange for your baptism.

We want to extend an invitation to church membership to Christians who are worshipping with us tonight. You also may use the common response slip to do this.

C. Attention

Question: What is your favorite Christmas movie?

189

My favorite is the movie: *It's a Wonderful Life*. It's the story of a man named George Bailey. George always tries to do the right thing no matter how difficult it may be.

But on Christmas Eve he finds himself facing prison for something he didn't do. So George runs. He finds himself on a bridge and is ready to plunge into the frigid waters.

That's when he encounters an unlikely angel by the name of Clarence. George tells Clarence that he wishes he had never been born. The angel seizes on that to show George that the world would have been a much sadder, darker place, if he hadn't lived.

Near the end of the film George again finds himself alone on bridge at the very spot where he was ready to commit suicide.

However something magical has happened to George. Clarence is gone but George is filled with an inexpressible joy. He runs back into town to be with his family. There are tears in his eyes. But these are not sad tears. They're tears of joy. George has gained a new understanding and appreciation for his life. Now he is joyous with the sights and sounds of Christmas.

Body of the Sermon

D. Problem/Need to be Resolved

Perhaps like George Bailey, some of us may have lost the joy of Christmas? Can we find it again as George Bailey did? Or have the cares of this year taken away any hope of Christmas joy? Will you answer honestly? Are you joyful this Christmas?

E. Biblical Solution to the Problem/Need

I believe the answer to Christmas joy is the same answer that was found by those who took part in that first Christmas. They too, were filled with fear and foreboding.

What was it that changed their fears into joy? An angel would appear to them with the good news that God was going to send a Savior. When the angel had departed they would discover that their fears had been replaced by joy.

It was true of Zechariah in the temple. It was true of Mary. It was true of Joseph. And it was true of the shepherds in the fields near Bethlehem.

Application

Now let's be clear. It wasn't the visit of the angel that caused fear to leave and joy to come. Often the appearance of an angel was initially a cause for fear. No, it was the message of the angel that brought joy.

Summary

What is the answer to finding our Christmas joy? It's the good news of that first Christmas. It's the message that God has sent the world a Savior who is Christ the Lord.

Transition

Tonight we're going to remember Christ's loving sacrifice for us by sharing The Lord's Supper. The Supper symbolizes the broken body and the shed blood of Christ given to save us from our sins.

Read and Briefly Explain: Matthew 26:17-30

The Passover was the yearly observance of the miracle that freed captive Israel from Egypt. They followed Moses to the home promised to them by God. (17)

Happier days of adulation and large crowds are coming to an end. Jesus and the disciples must be secretive. There is a plot to kill the Lord and scatter his disciples. (18-19)

The mood is somber. Then it becomes sorrowful. Jesus tells the twelve that the one who will betray him is among them. Every man considers the possibility that he might be the one who will fail the Lord. (20-25)

Judas becomes aware that Jesus knows that he is the one who will sell his friend and Lord. He leaves the table and goes out into the night to earn his thirty pieces of silver.

Jesus breaks the tradition of the Passover meal. He takes up the unleavened bread. Every head must have turned toward him. He blesses the bread. He breaks it. He gives it to them. (26)

Take – Take the suffering and sacrifice for your sins.

Eat - Internalize the cost of redemption. Become one with it.

This is my body – Look, think, and feel the love.

Jesus again breaks the tradition of the Passover observance by taking up the cup. He blesses it. He passes it. (27-28)

Drink from it – No hesitation or half-hearted response.

My blood – This is the new way to God. There's no other.

Remission – Sins will be forgiven because of this sacrifice.

The sacrificed body and blood of God's Son will usher in the Kingdom of God. It was this Kingdom that he came to establish. (29)

There's nothing left to do now. The Lamb must go to the place of sacrifice. The little band departs into the night. (30)

Summary

1. The Passover was from the hand of Moses. This is from the hand of the Son of God.

2. The Passover was made possible by the sacrifice of a lamb. This Communion was made possible by the sacrifice of the spotless Lamb of God.

3. The Passover was to set a people free from physical slavery. The body and blood of Christ was to set the world free from the slavery of Satan, sin, and death.

4. The observance of Passover identified those who belonged to Israel. The Communion observance identifies those who belong to the family of God.

Transition

If we rightly understand the love of Jesus Christ for us then we will find our Christmas joy. Listen carefully, and remember with me the events that followed that first Lord's Supper. Remember with me the events of the night and the following day, the day of crucifixion.

F. Visualization of the Solution

That night he was arrested in the garden and betrayed by Judas.

In the morning he was tried by a Jewish court and found guilty of blasphemy because he would not deny that he was the Son of God.

He was handed over to the Roman Governor, Pontius Pilate, for Roman judgment. He was beaten, mocked, and humiliated by the Roman soldiers. Finally he was condemned to death by Pilate.

He was forced to march to the place of execution carrying his cross. He fell beneath its weight.

At Golgotha he was nailed to the cross and raised between heaven and earth. His precious, redeeming blood flowed from the crown of thorns on his brow; from the wounds in his hands and feet, and from the whip-lashed wounds upon his back.

It was nine in the morning.

He forgave his accusers. He committed the care of his mother to John. He promised a dying but believing thief beside him that he would be with him in Paradise that very day.

Amazingly, at noon night fell upon the earth. He cried out for water. He called out to the Father in prayer.

He uttered his final words from the cross, "It is finished. Father, into thy hands I commend my spirit."

Then, he bowed his head and died.

Six hours had passed. In that brief time he had redeemed the world from sin.

Communion Observance: Serve the bread and the wine.

Arrange for appropriate music, instrumentally and/or vocally.

Conclusion to the Sermon

After Communion Summary

The message of Christmas is that God loves us. His son brings peace and joy to all who believe. Further, the message of Christmas is that peace and joy are possible even in the most difficult of circumstances. And the way to that peace and joy is through the realization and acceptance of his love.

G. Call for Response

Please take a moment to prayerfully look at the communion response slip. What is your response to the love of God through his son, Jesus? How will you respond to his sacrificial love for you?

Will you now prayerfully mark the slip and fold it once.

See the end of the sermon for a copy of, "My Communion Response to God's Love."

H. Invitation

As the instruments play the beautiful Christmas hymn, "Silent Night," please bring your communion response slip and place it on the communion table.

Alternative Invitation

As the ushers receive the Christmas Eve offering, please place your folded communion response slip in the offering plate to finalize your response to Christ's love.

I. Afterglow

The grace of the Lord Jesus Christ, and the love of God, and the fellowship of the Holy Spirit be with you. Peace and goodwill to all. Amen.

Note: Prior to the candlelight service reproduce the communion response slip in sufficient quantities. They are to be placed at the end of the pews. They should be passed at the beginning of the worship service.

My Communion Response to God's Love

___I repent of my sins and trust Jesus Christ as my Savoir and Lord. I want to be baptized into the membership of this Church.

___I want to transfer my church membership into this Church.

___I want to rededicate my life to Jesus Christ, my Lord.

___I want to surrender to God's call to the ministry.

___I believe God is speaking to me in the following way:

_____

Name: _____ Phone:_____ - _____ - _____

Chapter 20
Concluding Thoughts

I was a young minister in Illinois when I received my first bit of advice about preaching. It came from Carl Jacobs, a director of missions. He handed me a 3x5 index card upon which he had printed, "Preach as a dying man to dying men."

The card had an honored place taped to the corner of the pulpit. I would see it each time I preached. For 47 years I tried faithfully to preach and teach the wonderful message of the scriptures. Many of those messages were intended to be persuasive.

I doggedly used the traditional sermon form learned in college and affirmed in seminary. Obviously there were successes. But there were also failures as sermons yielded little or no visible results.

And then while in semi-retirement, out from under the demanding workload of a busy pastor, God began to help me understand how to better frame my message to accomplish the purpose of a persuasive sermon.

The process of developing this new sermon form was done over time by trial and error. The end result is the persuasive sermon form presented in this book. It's a new, innovative, and thoroughly tested sermon form.

Recently I was supplying at the First Baptist Church, Collinsville, Oklahoma, where I pastored for 23 years. After the message, a precious Christian lady and dear friend turned to my wife and said, "I think Brother Wana has become a better preacher since he retired." She was right.

The persuasive sermon form is an additional tool for any minister. It's designed to make the persuasive sermon more effective in accomplishing preaching goals.

It's my prayer for you that God will multiply the spiritual power of your preaching ministry through the persuasive sermon form.

The End

Also by Wana Archer

James Daniel and the First Christmas
A Christmas Journey

Now the whole family can experience the wonder of the first Christmas, wrapped up in a heartwarming story of love and redemption.

Travel to the first Christmas with James Daniel and the Queen. Fight off the savage attack of scavenger dogs. Rescue a Saluki pup from the fires of Gehenna. Foil roadside bandits and make friends with unlikely characters.

Along the way to Bethlehem, discover the sweetness of first love with James and the beautiful Jema

Then, experience the first Christmas in real time and historical detail, told with respectful awe. See this cosmic drama unfold through the eyes of Joseph and Mary, shepherds, angels and the Magi from the east.

Feel heaven's healing touch come down upon James as he cradles Mary's little son. Smile with the joy of the first Christmas.

The twenty-six chapters of *James Daniel and the First Christmas* are a perfect family read for the days of the Advent calendar.

Advent Edition
James Daniel and the First Christmas

Individuals and families can celebrate the days of Advent and also experience the wonder of the first Christmas through the pages of *James Daniel*.

Complete observances of the four Sundays of Advent and scripture readings for the days of the Advent calendar are incorporated into the chapter readings of the book.

The Answer: Solving the Science/Bible Problem

There's a cultural war raging between Secularists and Biblicists over what constitutes truth. This book analyzes the two sides of the controversy. It proposes a solution that honors both Bible and science.

A clear path to the reconciliation of scientific and biblical truths, free of scientific and theological language, is marked out for the reader to follow.

The place of faith and reason in living the truthful life is explained and offered for the reader's consideration.